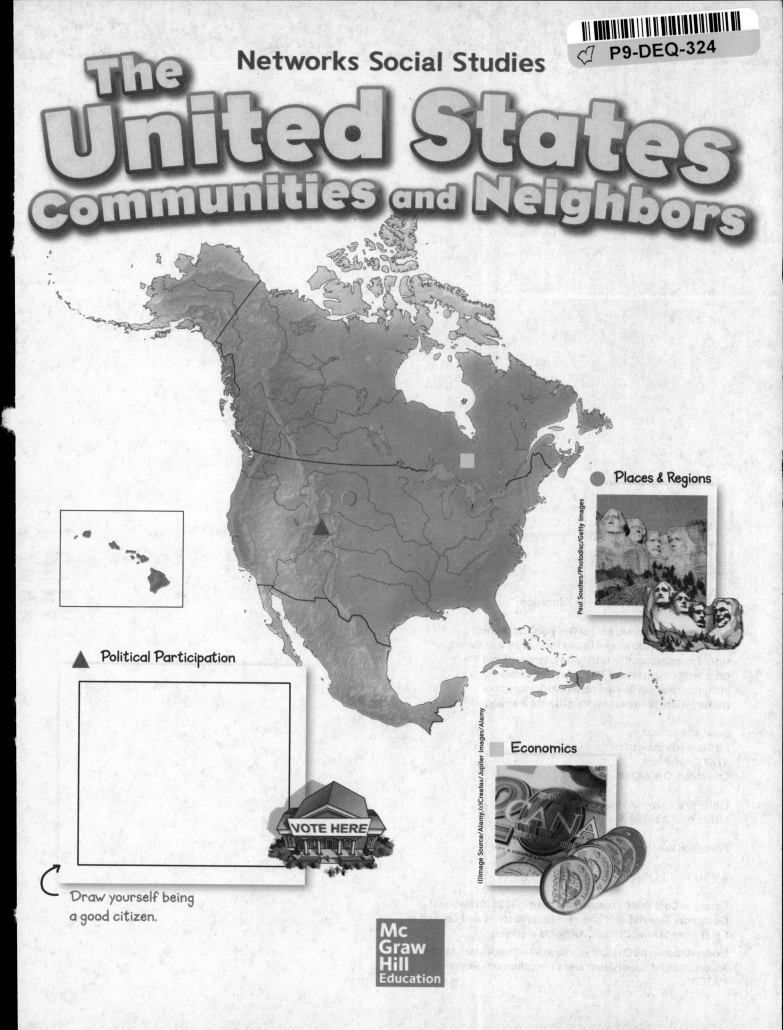

Networks Social Studies

The United States
Communities and Neighbors

Places & Regions

Paul Souders/Photodisc/Getty Images

Political Participation

VOTE HERE

Draw yourself being
a good citizen.

Economics

(l)Image Source/Alamy, (r)Creatas/Jupiter Images/Alamy

McGraw Hill Education

Send all inquiries to:
McGraw-Hill Education
8787 Orion Place
Columbus, OH 43240

ISBN: 978-0-02-130388-5
MHID: 0-02-130388-6

Printed in the United States of America.

8 9 10 11 12 QSX 23 22 21 20

PROGRAM AUTHORS

James A. Banks, Ph.D.
Kerry and Linda Killinger Endowed
    Chair in Diversity Studies and
    Director, Center for Multicultural
    Education
University of Washington
Seattle, Washington

Kevin P. Colleary, Ed.D.
Curriculum and Teaching Department
Graduate School of Education
Fordham University
New York, New York

Linda Greenow, Ph.D.
Associate Professor and Chair
Department of Geography
State University of New York at
    New Paltz
New Paltz, New York

Walter C. Parker, Ph.D.
Professor of Social Studies Education,
    Adjunct Professor of Political Science
University of Washington
Seattle, Washington

Emily M. Schell, Ed.D.
Visiting Professor, Teacher Education
San Diego State University
San Diego, California

Dinah Zike
Educational Consultant
Dinah-Might Adventures, L.P.
San Antonio, Texas

CONTRIBUTING AUTHORS

James M. Denham, Ph.D.
Professor of History and Director,
    Lawton M. Chiles, Jr., Center for
    Florida History
Florida Southern College
Lakeland, Florida

M.C. Bob Leonard, Ph.D.
Professor, Hillsborough Community
    College
Director, Florida History Internet Center
Ybor City, Florida

Jay McTighe
Educational Author and Consultant
McTighe and Associates Consulting
Columbia, Maryland

Timothy Shanahan, Ph.D.
Professor of Urban Education &
    Director, Center for Literacy
College of Education
University of Illinois at Chicago

ACADEMIC CONSULTANTS

Tom Daccord
Educational Technology Specialist
Co-Director, EdTechTeacher
Boston, Massachusetts

Joe Follman
Service Learning Specialist
Director, Florida Learn & Serve

Cathryn Berger Kaye, M.A.
Service Learning Specialist
Author, *The Complete Guide to
    Service Learning*

Justin Reich
Educational Technology Specialist
Co-Director, EdTechTeacher
Boston, Massachusetts

My Book

My Computer

networks™

Go online and find this interactive map of North America.

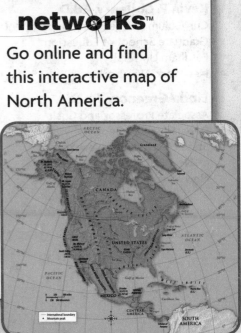

My Cover

Find something on the cover built by people. Describe what it is and explain why you think it is important.

_____

_____

_____

_____

EXplore! UNIT 2 Celebrating Culture

BIG IDEA 💡 Culture influences the way people live.

My Book

My Computer

networks™

Go online and find this
video about diversity
in the United States.

▶

My Cover

Find an activity on the cover that you have done or
would like to do. Draw a picture of yourself doing the
activity.

Keep going!
Next we'll explore
Economics!

EXplore! UNIT 3 Economics

BIG IDEA 💡 Economics affects people.

My Book

My Computer

networks™

Go online and find this video about economics.

My Cover

Find three pictures of money on the cover. In which countries did you find them? Write the countries on the lines.

_____

_____

_____

_____

EXplore! UNIT 4 Government and Civics

BIG IDEA: Rules provide order.

My Book

My Computer

networks™

Go online and find this video about our government.

Keep going! Next we'll explore Skills and Maps!

My Cover

Find a place on the cover where leaders meet. Describe what you think the leaders do there.

_____

_____

_____

_____

Explore! Skills and Maps

Skills

My Computer

networks™

Go online and find Skill Builders for more practice with Reading Skills and Primary Sources!

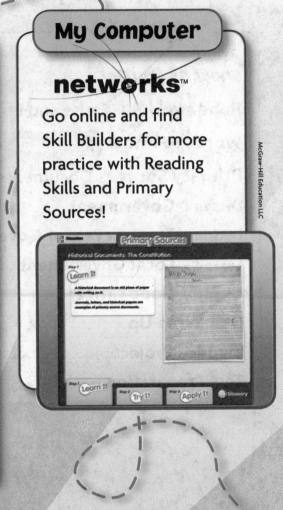

My Cover

Find three things on the cover you want to know more about. Draw or write about them here.

EXplore! Skills and Maps

Maps

My Computer

networks™

Go online and find this interactive map of the United States.

Reference Section

UNIT 1

The Geography of North America and the Caribbean

BIG IDEA Location affects how people live.

Every location on Earth is different. Some areas have low, flat land that is good for growing crops. Other areas have tall mountains, sandy deserts, or frozen ground where only certain plants will grow. What do you already know about the physical features of North America and the Caribbean? How do maps help us understand places on Earth? In this unit, you will read about the land in the United States and in our neighboring countries. As you read, think about how the location of a place affects the things that are living there.

Key
- Canada
- United States
- Mexico
- Caribbean

networks

There's More Online!
- Skill Builders
- Vocabulary Flashcards

Show As You Go! After you read each lesson, come back to these pages. After Lesson 1, label the countries and color the map. After the other lessons, fill in the boxes with information about the physical features, landmarks, climate, vegetation, and natural resources of each region. You will use your notes in a unit project later.

United States

_____

_____

_____

_____

_____

_____

Canada

_____

_____

_____

_____

_____

_____

Mexico

_____

_____

_____

_____

_____

_____

Caribbean

_____

_____

_____

_____

_____

_____

Reading Skill

Common Core Standards
RI.7 Use information gained from illustrations (e.g., maps, photographs) and the words in a text to demonstrate understanding of the text (e.g., where, when, why, and how key events occur).

Analyze Visuals

Have you ever heard the phrase, "A picture is worth a thousand words"? You can learn a lot of information by studying photographs, maps, and other images. Visuals like these can help you better understand what the text you are reading is telling you. They can also tell a story all on their own.

LEARN IT

- Look at the visual on this page. Ask, "What does this visual show?"

- As you read the text, look at the visual. Ask, "How does this visual help me understand what I am reading?"

- After you read, ask, "What extra information does this visual provide?"

The swamps of Louisiana are an important wetland area in the United States. It is home to many kinds of plants not found anywhere else in the country. Shallow ponds cover most of the swamps, providing hiding places for alligators.

The McGraw-Hill Companies - Inc./Barry Barker - photographer

This paragraph has information that is supported by the photograph.

This photograph illustrates the text in the paragraph. It also shows addtional information—an alligator living in the swamps of Louisiana.

TRY IT

You can make a list of details in paragraphs and photographs to help you understand what you are reading. Fill in the chart below with details from the paragraph and photograph on page 4. (Hint: You can underline information in the paragraph to help identify details.)

Details

APPLY IT

Use the photograph to complete the paragraph below about the dogwood tree.

The dogwood tree is Missouri's state tree. The flowers are the state flower of North Carolina. The dogwood tree also has

_____

that are white to pink.

What else does this picture tell you about the dogwood tree?

_____

_____

_____

_____

Words to Know

Common Core Standards
RI.4 Determine the meaning of general academic and domain-specific words and phrases in a text relevant to a grade 3 topic or subject area.

The list below shows some important words you will learn in this unit. Their definitions can be found on the next page. Read the words.

geography   (jee • AH • gruh • fee)

distortion   (dih • STAWR • shuhn)

elevation   (eh • luh • VAY • shuhn)

climate   (KLY • muht)

vegetation   (veh • juh • TAY • shuhn)

tundra   (TUHN • druh)

arable land   (A • ruh • buhl LAND)

arid   (A • ruhd)

FOLDABLES

The Foldable on the next page will help you learn these important words. Follow the steps below to make your Foldable.

Step 1   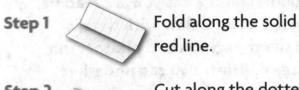   Fold along the solid red line.

Step 2   Cut along the dotted lines.

Step 3   Read the words and their definitions.

Step 4   Complete the activities on each tab.

Step 5   Look at the back of your Foldable. Choose ONE of these activities for each word to help you remember its meaning:

- Draw a picture of the word.

- Write a description of the word.

- Write how the word is related to something you know.

	FOLD
Geography is the study of Earth and the way living things use it.	Write a sentence that describes the geography where you live.
Distortion is when an object loses its original size and shape.	Write the two things that could change because of distortion. _____ _____
Elevation is the height of land above sea level.	Write a sentence using the word *elevation*.
Climate is the weather of a place over a long period of time.	Write two words that describe the climate where you live. _____ _____
Vegetation is the plants that grow in an area.	Write two words that are examples of vegetation. _____ _____
Tundra is a treeless plain where only grasses and mosses grow.	Circle the words that belong with the word *tundra*. tree moss fern grass cactus crop
Arable land is land that is good for farming.	Write the name of something that farmers could plant on arable land.
Arid means very dry.	Write an antonym for the word *arid*.

geography

distortion

elevation

climate

vegetation

tundra

arable land

arid

✂ CUT HERE

geography

distortion

elevation

climate

vegetation

tundra

arable land

arid

Historical Maps

Primary sources are written or made by someone who saw an event happen. They teach us about people, places, and events. A map is one type of primary source. A map is something that is used by people to learn more about a place on Earth. Maps that were made long ago can teach us about what a place was like in the past. You can analyze, or study, maps to learn more about places on Earth.

Look at this historical map. As you analyze the map, think about the details that tell you what this region was like in the past. The details tell you that the mapmaker explored this place long ago.

DBQ Document-Based Questions

Study the map. As you look at the details, answer the following questions.

1. **What detail tells you this map was made long ago?**

   _____

   _____

2. **How does this map look different from a map you would see today?**

   _____

networks
There's More Online!
● Skill Builders
● Resource Library

A Place in Our World

? Essential Question

Why is it important to know about where we live? What do you think?

_____

_____

_____

_____

Words To Know

Write a number on each line to show how much you know about the meaning of each word.

1 = I have no idea!

2 = I know a little.

3 = I know a lot!

____ **geography**

____ ***model**

____ **distortion**

____ **continent**

____ **landform**

____ **elevation**

Earth's Land and Water

Geography is the study of Earth and the way living things use it. You can read and look at pictures to learn about geography. You can also use a globe or a map. Can you find North America on a globe? What can a map tell you about a place? In this unit, you will learn about the physical geography of North America and the Caribbean. We will begin by looking at our world as a whole.

To understand where we live, let's look at a globe. A globe is a **model** of Earth. It shows Earth's land and water. A globe is a sphere. It is round, like a ball. You can only see half of a globe at a time. The part of the globe that you see is a hemisphere, which means "half of a sphere."

What do you see on the globe?

_____

_____

Like a globe, a map also shows Earth's land and water. However, a map is flat. When you look at a map of the world, you can see all the land and water on Earth at the same time.

If you stretched the surface of a globe to make it flat, like a map, you would change the size and shape of Earth's land and water. The shapes on Earth would be distorted. **Distortion** is when an object loses its original size and shape, like the boy in the picture on this page.

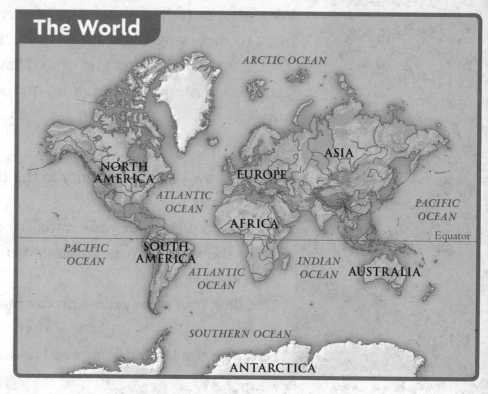

The World

ARCTIC OCEAN

NORTH AMERICA

ATLANTIC OCEAN

PACIFIC OCEAN

SOUTH AMERICA

ATLANTIC OCEAN

EUROPE

ASIA

AFRICA

PACIFIC OCEAN

Equator

INDIAN OCEAN

AUSTRALIA

SOUTHERN OCEAN

ANTARCTICA

Earth's land is divided into **continents**. A continent is a large area of land separated from other areas by water, mountains, or other natural features. There are seven continents on Earth. Can you name them?

The largest areas of water on Earth are called oceans. There are five oceans on Earth. Can you name the five oceans?

▼ **The boy's reflection is distorted.**

Look at the map above. Explain how it is distorted.

_____

_____

_____

_____

_____

_____

Where on Earth Are You?

We use maps to find places. The flow chart below uses different maps to show where you are. First, you live in a community in a state. States are part of the United States. The United States, Canada, and Mexico are countries on the continent of North America.

1. Draw your community in the blank box on the flow chart.
2. Draw a picture of your state. Draw a small x on the map to show where your community is located. Then color your state yellow.
3. Color your state yellow on the map of the United States, too.
4. Color the United States red on the map of North America.

Your Community

Your State

The United States

The World

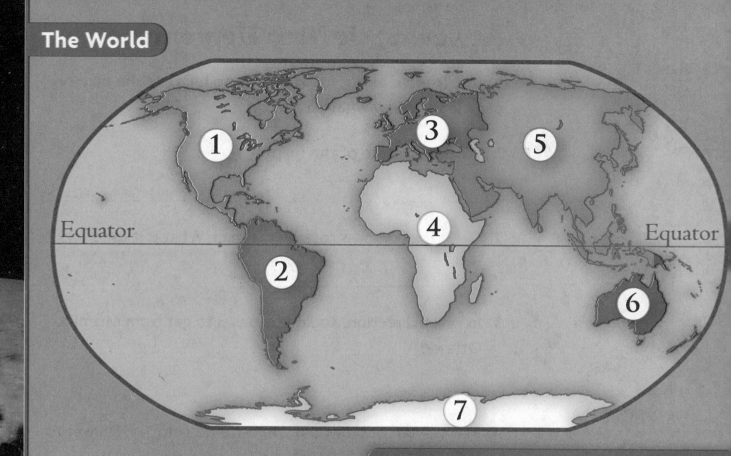

Equator

Equator

1
2
3
4
5
6
7

0   500   1,000 miles
0   500 1,000 kilometers

North America

Map and Globe Skills

1. Label the five oceans on the map of the world above.

2. Look at the numbers on the map. Write the names of the continents below.

Continents
1
2
3
4
5
6
7

13

Review Basic Map Elements

You've learned about maps before, so let's use the map on page 15 to review what you know!

1. What is the title of this map?

   _____

2. (Circle) the compass rose on the map. What is it used for?

   _____

3. In which direction would you travel to get from Miami to Ottawa?

   _____

4. In which direction would you travel to get from Denver to New Orleans?

   _____

5. Find the map scale on the map and label it. About how many miles is it from St. Louis to Chicago? San Francisco to Phoenix?

   St. Louis to Chicago is _____ miles.

   San Francisco to Phoenix is _____ miles.

6. Look at the numbers and letters on the grid. In which square is Edmonton, Canada?

   _____

7. Draw the symbol for national capitals used in the map legend.

14

Use a Political Map

Look at this map of North America. This is a political map. Political maps show borders, or the boundaries between places. Three of the largest countries in North America—Canada, the United States, and Mexico—are shown on the map. The Caribbean is shown on the map, too. The Caribbean is a group of islands near North America that is made up of small countries and commonwealths. A commonwealth is a territory that has its own government but also has strong ties to another nation. Puerto Rico and the Bahamas are both commonwealths.

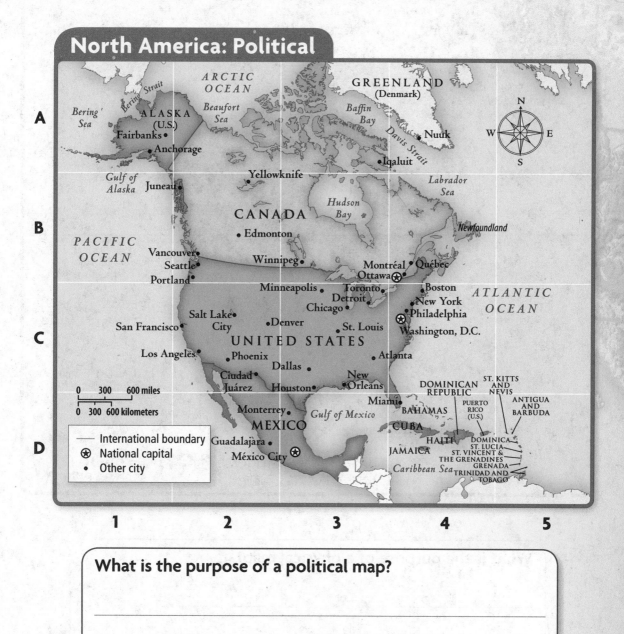

North America: Political

What is the purpose of a political map?

_____

_____

Use a Physical Map

Look at this map of North America. This is a physical map. Physical maps show **landforms**, or shapes on Earth's surface. Rivers, lakes, deserts, and mountains are all landforms. How can you tell the landforms apart? Mapmakers use different colors or shading for each landform. For example, water is usually blue, and areas around mountains are shaded.

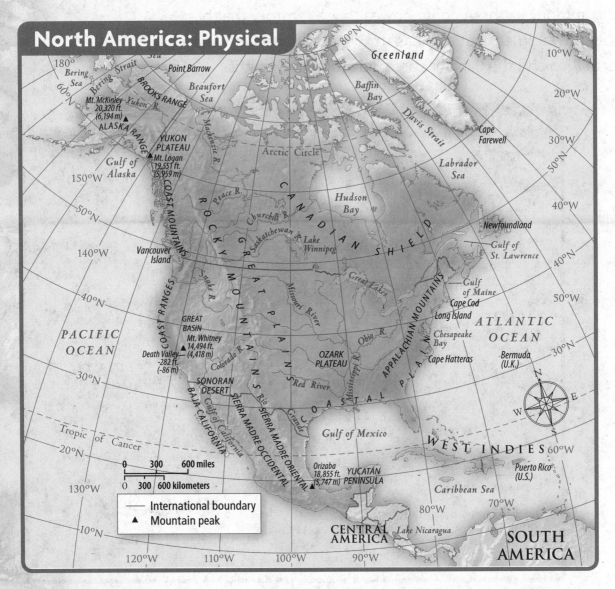

North America: Physical

What is the purpose of a physical map?

_____

_____

Use an Elevation Map

Have you ever wondered why the water in a river moves? The answer is because water runs downhill. Every river begins at a higher **elevation** than where it ends. Elevation is how high the land is above the sea. Elevation maps help us learn about the height of land. These maps use different colors to show land heights. The map key, also called a map legend, shows the colors that stand for different elevations.

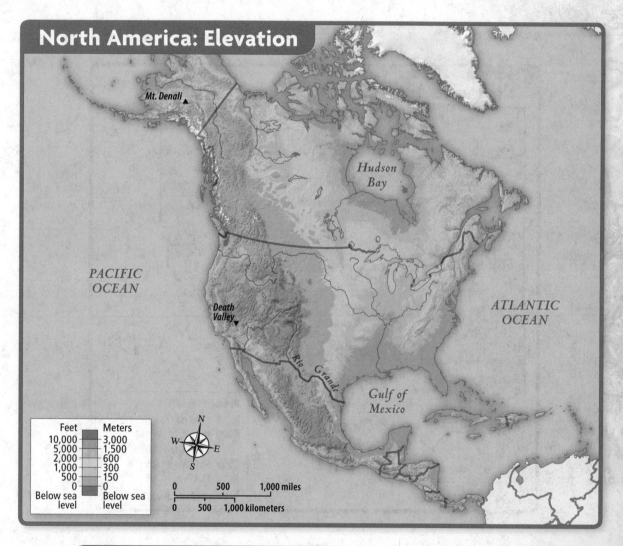

North America: Elevation

Mt. Denali ▲

Hudson Bay

PACIFIC OCEAN

Death Valley ▼

ATLANTIC OCEAN

Rio Grande

Gulf of Mexico

Feet	Meters
10,000	3,000
5,000	1,500
2,000	600
1,000	300
500	150
0	0
Below sea level	Below sea level

N
W · E
S

0   500   1,000 miles
0   500   1,000 kilometers

1. What is the purpose of an elevation map?

_____

_____

2. What is the range of elevation along the Gulf of Mexico?

_____

Use a Population Map

Another type of map is a population map. It shows how many people live in an area. Below is a population map of Ohio. As you can see, many people live in the area around Columbus. But some areas have a small population. Notice that the population is lower in northeast Ohio.

Population: Ohio

Number of People
- 1,000,000 to 1,280,122
- 300,000 to 999,999
- 100,000 to 299,999
- 50,000 to 99,999
- 13,435 to 49,999

Total State Population: 11,536,504

1. What is the purpose of this map?

_____

2. What type of map scale is used on this map?

_____

Use Map Scales

No matter what type of map you use, a map scale is a useful tool. A map scale shows the distance from one location to another. Mapmakers use different types of map scales to measure the distance between locations.

- A linear scale uses a straight line. Miles and kilometers are shown on the line. A linear scale is best to measure long distances, like the distance from Cincinnati to Cleveland.

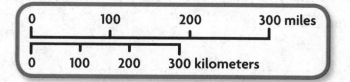

- A word scale—also called a language scale—actually has words in it! You might use a word scale if you are making a map of a city. For example, one inch on your map might be equal to one mile in the city.

1 inch equals 1 mile

- A fractional scale uses fractions, like 1/100. This type of scale would be useful if you were making a map of a small area, such as your classroom. One inch on your map might be equal to 100 inches in the classroom.

1/100 or 1:100

Circle the map scale you might use if you made a map of your city.

THINK · PAIR · SHARE
Think about how globes and maps help us understand where we live. Share your ideas with a partner.

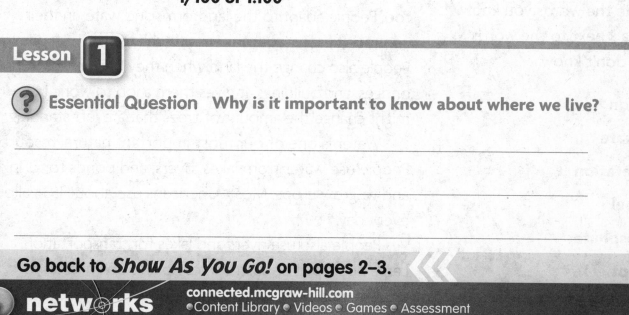

Lesson 1

? **Essential Question** Why is it important to know about where we live?

_____

_____

_____

Go back to *Show As You Go!* on pages 2–3.

The United States and Its Regions

What defines a region?
What do you think?

_____

_____

_____

_____

_____

_____

_____

Words To Know

Circle the words you know.
Put a ? next to the words
you don't know.

region

climate

vegetation

*label

phosphate

adapt

Pretend you have traveled to another country. When people ask you where you're from, how do you answer? Maybe you say, "I'm from the United States" or you name your state. The United States is a big country. It has 50 states, and not everyone knows where yours is located. How would you tell people where to find your state in the United States?

_____

_____

_____

_____

_____

Our country has many landforms, such as mountains, hills, valleys, and flat land. Landforms are part of geography, and they affect how people live. Water is part of geography, too. People adapt to the landforms and water in their communities. To **adapt** means to change the way you live. People also change the land when they build roads, tunnels, bridges, and buildings. It gives them a job to work, but might change the amount of trees that are left standing.

Water is one of our most important natural resources. People use water from lakes, rivers, and ponds for drinking and to grow crops. Most Americans use about 153 gallons every day.

People also use rivers and lakes for transportation. Large boats pull or push barges up and down rivers to move things from place to place. Rivers and lakes are useful for transportation, so many cities are located near rivers.

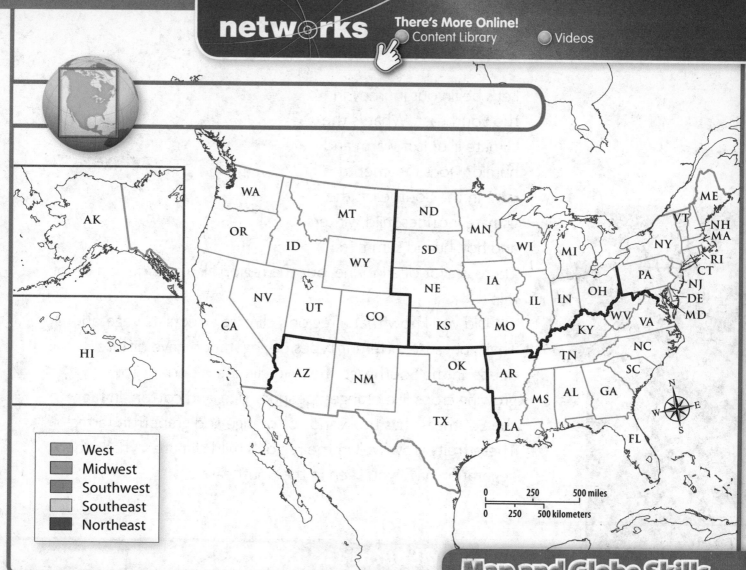

West
Midwest
Southwest
Southeast
Northeast

0   250   500 miles
0   250   500 kilometers

One Country, Five Regions

The United States is divided into five **regions**. A region is an area on Earth with common features that set it apart from other areas. The five geographic regions of the United States are the Southeast, the Northeast, the Midwest, the Southwest, and the West.

   Areas within a region usually share similar types of landforms. They share a common **climate**, too. Climate is the weather in a certain area over a period of time. Regions also have their own types of **vegetation**. Vegetation is the kinds of plants that grow in an area. Regions have landmarks, which are important places or objects. Landmarks can be natural or man-made. In this lesson, you will learn about the climate, vegetation, landmarks, and other physical features of each region of the United States.

Map and Globe Skills

1. Write a title for this map.

2. Use the map key to color each region.

3. In which region is California

_____

The Southeast

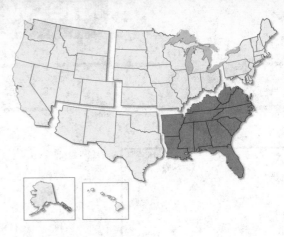

Let's begin our journey in the Southeast. What is the climate like? Is it warm and humid? Does it sometimes rain? In the Southeast, the climate includes mild winters and hot, humid summers. There is a lot of sunshine, but the region also gets quite a bit of rain.

Did you know that a region's climate affects its vegetation? That's because different types of vegetation have different needs. In the Southeast, the mild climate is perfect for growing crops like oranges, peanuts, rice, and cotton. In fact, the Southeast has thousands of orange and grapefruit farms! These fruits grow well in the region's mild climate. What other vegetation have you seen in the Southeast?

Creatas Images

▲ Oranges grow well in the Southeast's mild climate.

Map and Globe Skills

1. **Label** the states in the Southeast.

2. Use the map to describe the physical features of the Southeast.

_____

_____

_____

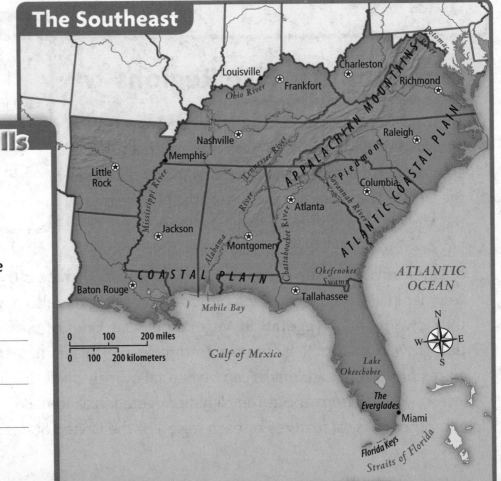

The Southeast

Natural Resources and Landmarks

The Southeast has many natural resources. A natural resource is found in nature and is used by people. Coal mined in the Southeast is used in power plants. This coal helps create half of our country's electricity! Trees found in the Southeast are an important natural resource, too. Cedar trees are used to make fences. **Phosphate** is also found in the Southeast. Phosphate is a mineral that farmers use to help crops grow. The Southeast is one of the world's largest producers of phosphate.

The Southeast has landmarks, too. Landmarks can be natural or man-made. One natural landmark in the region is the Florida Everglades. The Everglades is one of the largest wetland areas on Earth. The Cape Henry Lighthouse is an example of a man-made landmark. This lighthouse was built along the Atlantic Coast in Virginia over 200 years ago. Its light helped guide ships along the coast of our new nation!

(c) T. O'Keefe/PhotoLink/Getty Images, (cr) SuperStock/SuperStock, (b) Iconotec / Alamy

Underline the natural resources that come from the Southeast.

Phosphate is a natural resource. ▶

▼ The Everglades is a natural landmark in the Southeast.

▲ The Cape Henry Lighthouse is on the coast of Virginia.

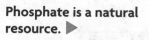

The Northeast

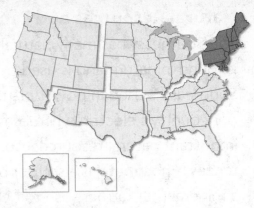

Now let's look at the Northeast. The climate of the Northeast is different from the climate of the Southeast. The Northeast has cold, snowy winters and rainy springs. Summers can be very hot or mild, depending on the year. Since the region is close to the Atlantic Ocean, it gets plenty of precipitation all year long. Precipitation is the moisture in the air that falls to the ground, such as rain and snow.

All of this precipitation helps the vegetation in the area. The region is full of forests. Some trees, such as pine trees, stay green all year long. Other trees, such as maple and oak trees, have leaves that change color in the autumn. Other vegetation in the region includes apple trees and crops, such as pumpkins.

flickr RF/Getty Images

Reading Skill

Compare and Contrast

To compare means to explain how things are similar. To contrast means to explain how things are different. Use the graphic organizer below to compare and contrast the resources found in the Northeast and those found in the Southeast.

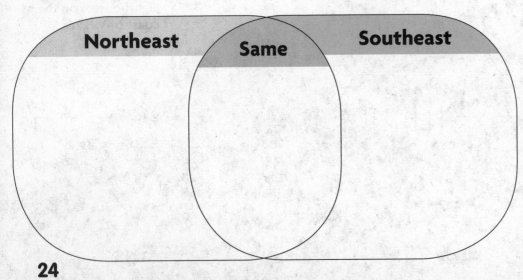

Northeast	Same	Southeast

Resources and Landmarks

Trees are one of the region's important natural resources. They are used to make items like furniture, paper, and pencils. The Atlantic Ocean is another natural resource in the Northeast. Most of our country's lobsters come from the cold Atlantic waters. These waters also provide crabs, oysters, and fish for our restaurants and dinner tables. Other natural resources found in the Northeast include granite and marble. Granite is used to make kitchen countertops.

Did you know that the Northeast has one of the country's largest waterfalls? Niagara Falls is a group of waterfalls on the border of the United States and Canada. This natural landmark runs power plants that provide electricity to thousands of people in the Northeast and parts of Canada. More than 750,000 gallons of water rushes over the Falls every second! The Northeast has man-made landmarks, too. One example is the Statue of Liberty located on the east coast of New York. This landmark is a well-known symbol for freedom.

PhotoLink/Getty Images

Write a caption for this picture.

_____

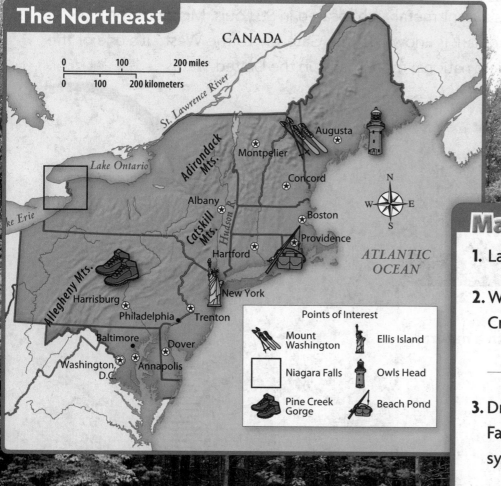

The Northeast

CANADA

0   100   200 miles

0   100   200 kilometers

St. Lawrence River

Lake Ontario

Adirondack Mts.

Augusta

Montpelier

Concord

Albany

Catskill Mts.

Hudson R.

Boston

Providence

Hartford

ATLANTIC OCEAN

Allegheny Mts.

Harrisburg

Philadelphia   Trenton

New York

Baltimore   Dover

Washington, D.C.   Annapolis

Lake Erie

N W E S

Points of Interest

Mount Washington   Ellis Island

Niagara Falls   Owls Head

Pine Creek Gorge   Beach Pond

Map and Globe Skills

1. Label the states in the Northeast.

2. What symbol represents Pine Creek Gorge in Pennsylvania?

_____

3. Draw a symbol for Niagara Falls in the map key. Draw your symbol on the map, too!

25

The Midwest

A third region in the United States is the Midwest. Four of the Great Lakes are found in the Midwest. These freshwater lakes are important natural landmarks in this region. They also affect the region's climate. In the winter, winds pick up moisture from the lakes. The moisture mixes with the cold air to create snow. Many cities near the Great Lakes get a lot of snow in the winter. Like the Northeast, summers can be hot or mild, depending on the year.

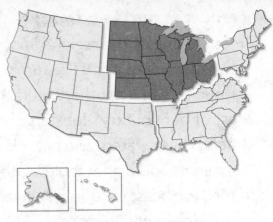

Landmarks

The Midwest has many interesting man-made landmarks. One of the most famous is Mount Rushmore in South Dakota. It took workers almost 15 years to carve the faces of four Presidents of the United States into the mountainside.

The Gateway Arch is another well-known Midwest landmark. It is a giant metal arch located in St. Louis, Missouri. This landmark is known as "the Gateway to the West." It's one of the tallest national monuments in the United States.

▼ **Mount Rushmore**

▲ **Gateway Arch**

Reading Skill

Analyze Visuals

Why is Mount Rushmore both a natural and a man-made landmark?

_____

_____

The Midwest

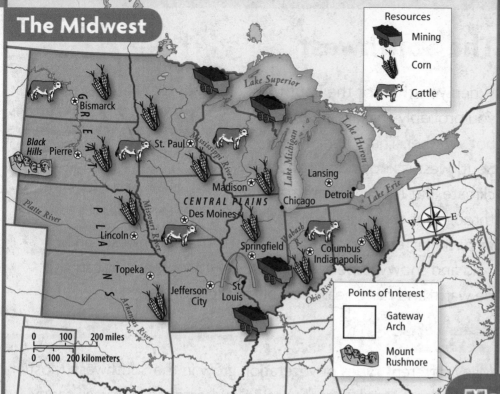

Resources
- Mining
- Corn
- Cattle

Lake Superior · Lake Michigan · Lake Huron · Lake Erie

Bismarck · GREAT · St. Paul · Mississippi River
Black Hills · Pierre · Madison · Lansing · Detroit
CENTRAL PLAINS · Chicago
Des Moines · Platte River · Missouri River
Lincoln · Springfield · Columbus · Indianapolis · Wabash R.
Topeka · Jefferson City · St. Louis · Ohio River

P L A I N S · Arkansas River

0 100 200 miles
0 100 200 kilometers

Points of Interest
- Gateway Arch
- Mount Rushmore

Resources and Vegetation

The land between the Appalachian and Rocky
Mountains is known as the Great Plains. Much of the
Midwest lies in this area of low, flat grassland. The
soil here is very rich and is one of the region's most
important resources. It makes the land great for farming!
Crops such as wheat, corn, and soybeans are grown
on farms throughout the Midwest. Cattle, pigs, and
chickens are raised on farms throughout the region, too.

Another natural resource found in the Midwest is iron ore.
Iron ore is used to make steel. Steel is used to make cars, bridges,
and buildings. In fact, steel was used to make the Gateway Arch!

Map and Globe Skills

1. Label the states in the Midwest.

2. Add the symbol for the Gateway Arch to the map key.

3. Circle all the symbols for crops on the map.

The Southwest

When you think of the Southwest, you probably think of deserts and hot weather. That's because the Southwest is known for its hot, dry climate. But if you were to travel throughout the region, you'd want to pack mittens and an umbrella, too! The Southwest can be cold and snowy, especially in the Rocky Mountains. It can also be warm and rainy near the Gulf of Mexico.

Vegetation

Many different types of vegetation grow in the Southwest. Most of the plants that live in the region's deserts can survive in sandy soil and on a limited amount of water. The saguaro, a giant cactus found in the Southwest, stores water in its trunk. It has a thick, tough skin and can survive the long dry season. Wildflowers do well in areas that get more water. Pine trees grow well in the region's colder climates.

Landmarks

The Southwest is also home to the Grand Canyon. This canyon is one of our country's most famous natural landmarks. The canyon is very deep, has steep sides, and stretches for 277 miles. It was formed by the Colorado River over thousands of years. One of the largest dams ever built in the United States—the Glen Canyon Dam—is also in the Southwest. This man-made landmark generates electricity that powers several states in the region.

1. **Write captions for the pictures.**
2. <u>Underline</u> **why the Glen Canyon Dam is important to the Southwest.**

The Southwest

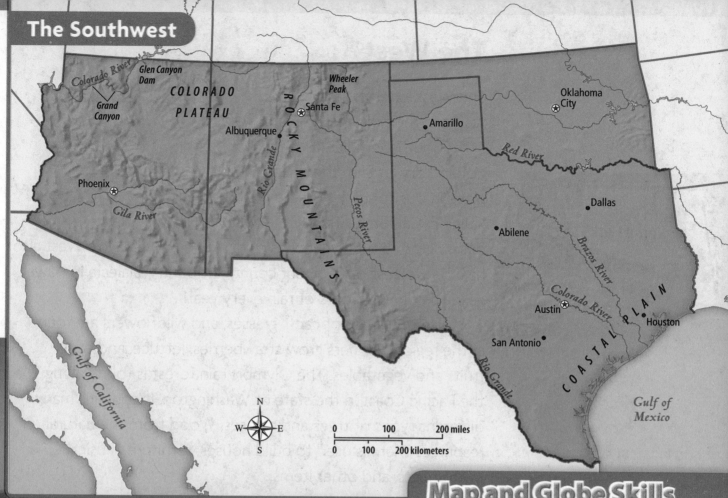

Natural Resources

The Southwest has several important natural resources, too. Minerals such as copper, silver, and uranium are mined from the ground. Another natural resource of the Southwest is oil. Workers drill deep into the earth and pipe oil up to the surface. Texas, the largest state in the Southwest, produces more oil than any other state in the country!

Map and Globe Skills

1. Label the states in the Southwest.

2. In which direction would you travel to get from Glen Canyon Dam to Wheeler Peak?

_____

The West

The West extends from Alaska in the north to Hawaii in the south. Some areas are hot and dry. In fact, the driest place in our country is Death Valley in California. This desert gets about two inches of rainfall each year! The West also has the wettest place in our country. Mount Waialeale in Hawaii gets almost 500 inches of rain every year!

Different types of cacti, grasses, and wildflowers are found in the region. Farmers grow strawberries, lettuce, and other fruits and vegetables. The Olympic rain forest is found along the Pacific Coast in the state of Washington. It contains many different types of trees and mosses. Wood from the natural resources there is used to build houses, furniture, musical instruments, and other items.

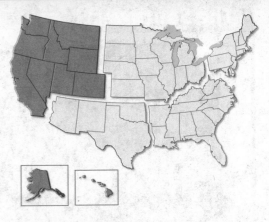

Map and Globe Skills

1. Label the states in the West.

2. Which ocean is north of Alaska?

_____

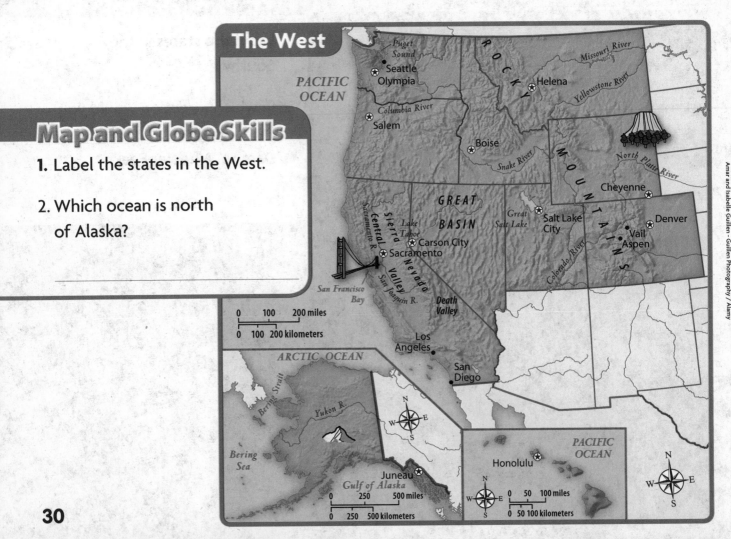

The West

PACIFIC OCEAN

Puget Sound
Seattle
Olympia
Columbia River
Salem
Boise
Snake River

ROCKY

Missouri River
Helena
Yellowstone River

MOUNTAINS

North Platte River
Cheyenne

GREAT BASIN
Great Salt Lake
Salt Lake City
Denver
Vail
Aspen
Colorado River

Sierra Nevada
Central Valley
Sacramento R.
Lake Tahoe
Carson City
Sacramento

San Francisco Bay
San Joaquin R.
Death Valley

Los Angeles
San Diego

0   100   200 miles
0   100   200 kilometers

ARCTIC OCEAN
Bering Strait
Yukon R.
Bering Sea
Juneau
Gulf of Alaska
0   250   500 miles
0   250   500 kilometers

PACIFIC OCEAN
Honolulu
0   50   100 miles
0   50 100 kilometers

Landmarks

What's the highest point in North America? The answer is Mount Denali. This natural landmark in Alaska is 20,320 feet above sea level! Another natural landmark in the West is Devils Tower in Wyoming. This national monument may have been formed by an ancient volcano. One of the most famous man-made landmarks in the United States is the Golden Gate Bridge. Millions of people travel to San Francisco, California, from all over the world to visit the bridge each year.

> **Use the information in the paragraph to label the pictures above.**

Describe the vegetation in the West.

_____

_____

Lesson 2

? Essential Question What defines a region?

_____

_____

_____

Go back to *Show As You Go!* on pages 2–3. ◀◀◀

netw⊙rks **connected.mcgraw-hill.com**
● Games   ● Assessment

Canada

32-33 (bkgd) SuperStock/age fotostock

? Essential Question

How are places unique and different?

What do you think?

_____

_____

_____

_____

_____

_____

Words To Know

Find out what the last two words mean. Write the name of a plant to go with each word.

*locate
tundra

_____

arable land

_____

Our Northern Neighbor

Canada is the largest country on the continent of North America. It is north of the United States. Oceans surround Canada on the east, west, and north. Canada has very tall, jagged mountains in the west and lower, more rounded mountains in the east. The land in the middle has plains and grasslands. There are also many forests, rivers, and lakes. In fact, Canada shares four of the Great Lakes with the United States.

The map and pictures on theses pages show some of the different landforms in Canada. Can you **locate** the Rocky Mountains and the Great Plains on the map?

▼ Great Plains

What landforms do the United States and Canada share?

_____

_____

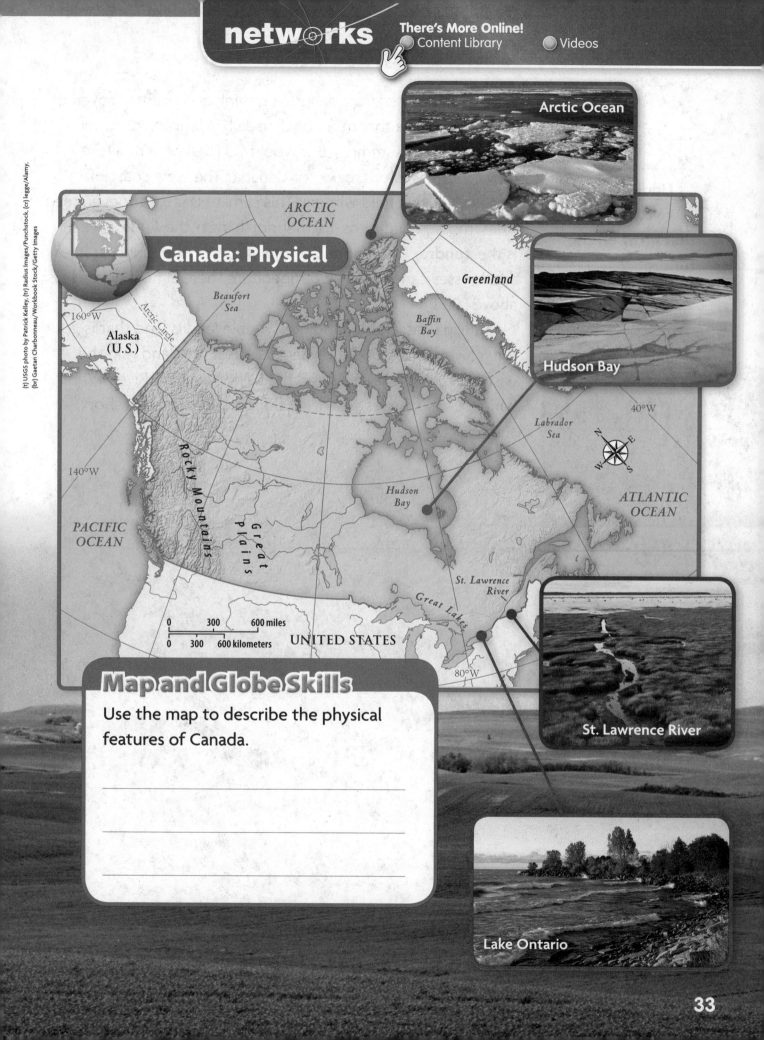

Arctic Ocean

Canada: Physical

ARCTIC OCEAN

Greenland

Hudson Bay

Beaufort Sea

Baffin Bay

160°W

Arctic Circle

Alaska (U.S.)

Labrador Sea

40°W

140°W

Rocky Mountains

Great Plains

Hudson Bay

ATLANTIC OCEAN

PACIFIC OCEAN

St. Lawrence River

Great Lakes

0   300   600 miles

0   300   600 kilometers

UNITED STATES

80°W

Map and Globe Skills

Use the map to describe the physical features of Canada.

_____

_____

_____

St. Lawrence River

Lake Ontario

Climate and Vegetation

Underline two things that grow on the tundra.

When you think of Canada, do you think of a country covered in snow? It's true that most of Canada has long, cold winters and short, cool summers. But would you believe a rain forest grows in the western region of Canada? The west coast of Canada has wet, mild winters. This climate is great for evergreen trees, mosses, and ferns. Farther north, near the Arctic Ocean, is the **tundra**. The tundra is a treeless plain where only grasses and mosses can grow. The temperature there almost never gets above 50°F!

Canada has **arable land**, too. Arable land is land that is good for growing crops. Some of Canada's best farmland is in the east near the Great Lakes and the Saint Lawrence River. Wheat, barley, and soybeans grow well there during Canada's short summers.

▼ **Rain forest**

▼ Tundra

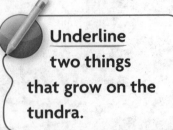

Canada's Resources

The forests in Canada are one of the country's most important resources. Trees are used to build houses and make paper. Did you know that a lot of the paper that newspapers are printed on comes from Canada? Canada is rich with other resources, too. Parts of eastern Canada have large iron-ore deposits. As you learned in Lesson 2, iron ore is used to make steel. Other mineral resources mined in Canada include gold, copper, silver, and nickel. Some of the energy resources found in Canada are coal, oil, and natural gas. Most of Canada's natural gas is east of the Rocky Mountains.

▲ Oil pipelines

> **How are Canada's resources similar to the resources of the United States?**
>
> _____
>
> _____

Canada's Natural Resources

ARCTIC OCEAN

Greenland

Beaufort Sea

Alaska (U.S.)

Baffin Bay

PACIFIC OCEAN

Hudson Bay

Labrador Sea

Vancouver • Calgary

Winnipeg

St. John's

Montréal • Halifax

Ottawa

Toronto

UNITED STATES

ATLANTIC OCEAN

Legend
- Coal
- Copper
- Gold
- Natural gas
- Nickel
- Oil
- Silver

N
W E
S

0   300   600 miles
0   300   600 kilometers

Map and Globe Skills

Which two natural resources are found near Hudson Bay?

1. _____

2. _____

Horseshoe Falls on
the Niagara River ▶

Natural and Man-Made Landmarks

As you learned in Lesson 2, Niagara Falls is on the border between the United States and Canada. This natural landmark is a series of three huge waterfalls. The Horseshoe Falls is the part of the falls that is in Canada. Another natural landmark in Canada is the Bay of Fundy. It is an inlet in eastern Canada along the Atlantic Ocean. Most areas along the coast of the bay experience very high and very low tides. Tides are the rise and fall of the ocean water.

Draw the way you think the Bay of Fundy looks at high tide in the empty box on the right.

▲ Bay of Fundy at low tide

▲ Bay of Fundy at high tide

(t) Glen Allison/Getty Images, (b) Image Ideas / PictureQuest

Canada has many man-made landmarks, too. One of the most famous is Parliament Hill in Ottawa, the capital of Canada. Many of Canada's government leaders work in this building. It was built over 150 years ago! Other man-made landmarks include the Calgary Tower in Calgary and the CN Tower in Toronto.

▲ Parliament Hill

How is Parliament Hill like a building in your community?

_____

_____

_____

Lesson 3

? Essential Question How are places unique and different?

_____

_____

_____

_____

_____

_____

Go back to *Show As You Go!* on pages 2–3.

netw⦿rks connected.mcgraw-hill.com
• Games   • Assessement

38-39 (bkgd) Marco Regalia/Alamy, (b) Kristi J. Black/Corbis

(?) Essential Question

How are places unique and different?
What do you think?

_____

_____

_____

_____

_____

_____

Words To Know

Tell a partner what you already know about these words.

peninsula
plateau
arid
*recall

Our Southern Neighbor

The United States and Canada aren't the only countries on North America. Mexico is located on the continent, too! Mexico is south of the United States. Large bodies of water surround Mexico to the west and the east. If you look at the map, you will see that the country's shape is curved, like a giant fish hook.

Most of Mexico's coastline has low elevations. But Mexico has high elevations, too. Mountains stretch along the west near the Pacific Ocean, and inland from the Gulf of Mexico in the east. Some of Mexico's highest mountains are volcanoes. Each picture on these pages has a number. The numbers on the map show where to find the landforms shown in the pictures.

Popocatépetl is an active volcano in southern Mexico. 1

Mexico has two large **peninsulas**. A peninsula is an area of land mostly surrounded by water. The Baja Peninsula is between the Pacific Ocean and the Gulf of California. The coastline of the Yucatan Peninsula, shown here, is in the Gulf of Mexico. 2

Mexico: Elevation

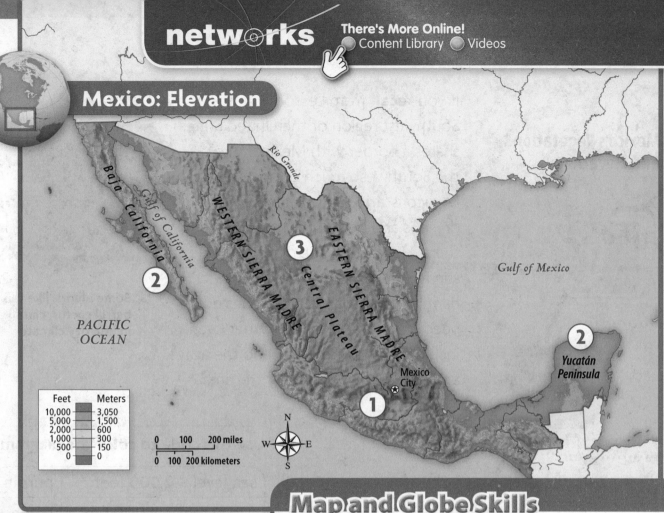

Baja California

Gulf of California

Rio Grande

WESTERN SIERRA MADRE

EASTERN SIERRA MADRE

Central Plateau

3

2

PACIFIC
OCEAN

Gulf of Mexico

2

Yucatán
Peninsula

Mexico
City

1

Feet	Meters
10,000	3,050
5,000	1,500
2,000	600
1,000	300
500	150
0	0

0   100   200 miles

0   100   200 kilometers

N
W   E
S

Gordon Sinclair/Alamy

The Rio Grande is a river that begins in the United States and flows into the Gulf of Mexico. It makes up much of the border between the United States and Mexico. Can you find the Rio Grande on the map?

Map and Globe Skills

1. What type of map is shown here?

_____

2. Which landform has a higher elevation, the Central Plateau or the Yucatan Peninsula?

_____

Mexico's largest land area is a **plateau**. A plateau is a high, flat area of land. The Central Plateau is shown here. It lies between the Western and Eastern Sierra Madre, which are two mountain ranges in Mexico.

3

Climate and Vegetation

If you **recall** from Lesson 2, the Southwest region of the United States shares a border with Mexico. Like the Southwest, much of northern Mexico is **arid**. Arid means very dry. It is arid because little rain falls there. However, some plants are able to survive in this type of environment. The barrel cactus, for example, does not need much water to live. Other cacti, including the prickly pear and the agave, are also found throughout the area.

▲ Some plants, like this barrel cactus, can survive in hot, dry climates.

Mexico's Vegetation and Elevation

moss
above 10,000 feet

forest
8,000 feet – 10,000 feet

apples
6,000 feet – 8,000 feet

coffee
4,000 feet – 6,000 feet

beans
2,000 feet – 4,000 feet

bananas
sea level – 2,000 feet

Use this code to color the diagram.

sea level – 2,000 feet	purple
2,000 feet – 4,000 feet	green
4,000 feet – 6,000 feet	red
6,000 feet – 8,000 feet	orange
8,000 feet – 10,000 feet	yellow
above 10,000 feet	white

Which plants grow best above 8,000 feet?

_____

_____

Climate isn't the only thing that affects the vegetation in Mexico. The land in Mexico has many different elevations. You learned in Lesson 1 that elevation is the height of land above sea level. Certain types of plants grow well at different elevations. Some plants grow well at sea level. Other plants grow well in the mountains. What does the diagram on page 40 tell you about Mexico's vegetation and elevation?

Mexico's Resources

Did you know that Mexico is one of the largest producers of silver in the world? Silver is used to make jewelry, such as rings and necklaces. It is also used in televisions and in cell phones. Copper and gold are other natural resources found in Mexico. Copper is used to make pipes. Like silver, gold is used to make jewelry. It is also used by dentists to fix teeth! Other resources, such as natural gas and oil, are found in Mexico, too. Mexico is one of the world's top producers of oil.

▲ A ring made with silver

Chart and Graph Skills

Reading Bar Graphs

Bar graphs use bars to display and compare information. Read the information in the box. Add bars to this graph for the United States, Canada, and Mexico.

> **United States—9 million barrels**
>
> **Canada—2 million barrels**
>
> **Mexico—3 million barrels**

How many more barrels of oil per day does Mexico produce than Canada?

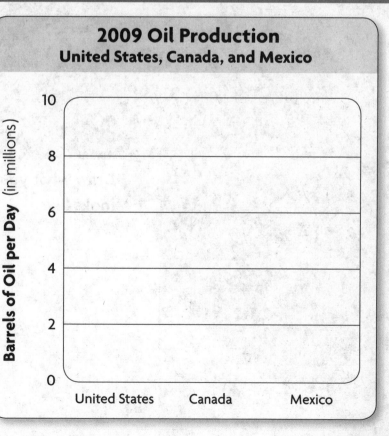

2009 Oil Production
United States, Canada, and Mexico

Barrels of Oil per Day (in millions)

10

8

6

4

2

0

United States   Canada   Mexico

The McGraw-Hill Companies Inc./Ken Cavanagh Photographer

Mexico's Landmarks

Have you ever seen a rock that looked like an animal or a plant? Mexico has many of these kinds of rocks. It takes a long time for these natural landmarks to be created. The unusual shapes are formed when sand blows across the surface of the rocks. The blowing sand wears away the softer rock. The harder rock does not wear away as fast, which forms these shapes.

Mexico has other natural landmarks, too. Copper Canyon is located in the Western Sierra Madre mountain range. This canyon is deeper than the Grand Canyon in the United States! The canyon was carved out by the rivers that flow through it. Copper Canyon gets its name from the copper mines in the area.

▼ Valley of Frogs

Marco Regalia / Alamy

Draw what you think the Valley of Mushrooms looks like.

▼ El Angel

Rocks and canyons aren't Mexico's only landmarks. In the center of Mexico City stands El Angel. This man-made landmark was built to celebrate the country's freedom from Spain. Other man-made landmarks in Mexico include temples and pyramids. These landmarks were built by the Maya, one of Mexico's first people. These ancient landmarks can still be found throughout Mexico today.

Maya pyramid ▶

Lesson 4

? Essential Question How are places unique and different?

_____

_____

_____

_____

_____

_____

Go back to *Show As You Go!* on pages 2–3. ◀◀

netw⊙rks
connected.mcgraw-hill.com
• Games • Assessment

The Caribbean

How are places unique and different?
What do you think?

_____

_____

_____

_____

_____

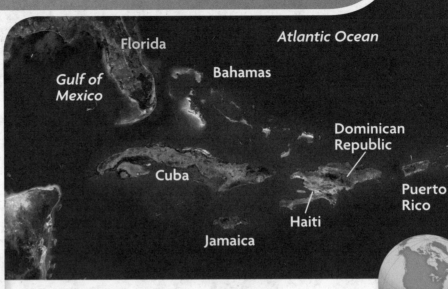

Florida   Atlantic Ocean

Gulf of Mexico   Bahamas

Cuba   Dominican Republic

Haiti   Puerto Rico

Jamaica

Planet Observer / Universal Images Group/Getty Images

Words To Know

Draw the symbol next to each word to show how much you know about the meaning of the word.

? = I have no idea!
▲ = I know a little.
★ = I know a lot.

_____ **satellite image**

_____ **humidity**

_____ **maritime climate**

_____ ***pattern**

Land in Blue Waters

The Caribbean is a region of islands off the coast of Florida. There are many countries in the Caribbean. The countries of Haiti and the Dominican Republic share the island of Hispaniola. Jamaica and Cuba are countries in the Caribbean, too. The Bahamas is a group of many small islands. Together, the islands of the Bahamas form a commonwealth. Another commonwealth in the Caribbean is Puerto Rico. As you learned in Lesson 1, a commonwealth is a territory that has its own government but also has strong ties to another nation. Puerto Rico is a commonwealth of the United States.

Look at the **satellite image**—or a picture of Earth taken from space—above. It shows the countries and commonwealths of the Caribbean. Do you see how close Florida is to the islands of the Caribbean?

1. Draw a circle around Jamaica in the picture above.

2. How is this satellite image like a map?

_____

_____

This is Emilio. He and his family recently traveled to the Caribbean. Read his journal, and use it to answer the questions.

Two Days in Jamaica

Stockbyte/Getty Images

Day 1

We are in Jamaica. It is humid here. **Humidity** is the amount of water vapor in the air. My skin feels sticky and hot. We are on our way to the hotel.

Day 2

Today we played on the beach. The sand was hot under my bare feet. I took a picture of this plant with the beautiful red flowers. It is called a hibiscus.

Write a caption for the picture above.

Reading Skill

Analyze Text and Visuals

1. Where did Emilio go with his family? _____

2. Why does his skin feel sticky? _____

3. What kind of plant is in the picture? _____

45

Climate and Vegetation

Like Emilio, many people from around the world vacation in the Caribbean. One reason is because of its **maritime climate**. Maritime climate is climate controlled by a large body of water, such as an ocean. The climate **pattern** in the Caribbean is mild all year long. The days are warm no matter what time of year it is.

Sometimes small afternoon storms blow in from the ocean. These are short storms with lots of rain. Sometimes the Caribbean gets hit with large storms called hurricanes. Hurricanes are dangerous storms. These storms pick up moisture and gain strength as they move over the warm water of the Caribbean. The heavy rains can cause flooding. Strong winds can blow the roof off a house. It would not be a good time to vacation in the Caribbean during a hurricane!

> **How is the climate of the Caribbean like the climate in your state?**
>
> _____
>
> _____

▼ **Hurricane winds can destroy homes.**

Like other places we have learned about, the Caribbean is home to many kinds of vegetation. The forests of the Caribbean have both broadleaf and evergreen trees. Plants such as ferns and mosses grow on the edge of these forests. Citrus fruit such as grapefruit, lemons, and limes grow well in the Caribbean, too. People in the Caribbean also grow bananas, coconuts, coffee, and sugarcane. Maybe you have eaten a banana that was grown in the Caribbean!

Sugarcane ▶

Draw a picture of a plant that grows well in the Caribbean. Write a caption for your picture.

Natural Resources

Natural resources are found in each country and commonwealth of the Caribbean. Some of the resources are unique, but many are the same. Trees are one of the Caribbean's natural resources. There aren't as many forests today as long ago, though. Much of the Caribbean's forests have been cut down and used by people.

The chart below shows some of the other natural resources found in the Caribbean. Use the chart to answer the questions.

▼ Rock salt

Country or Commonwealth	Natural Resource	How It Is Used
Puerto Rico	fish	to make sandwiches
Cuba	nickel	to make computer parts
Bahamas	sand	to build brick buildings
Dominican Republic	rock salt	to make ice cream
Haiti	cocoa	to make soap
Jamaica	bauxite	to make aluminum cans

Chart and Graph Skill

1. Which natural resource is used to build brick buildings?

_____

2. In which country is bauxite mined?

_____

3. How is nickel used?

_____

4. How do natural resources benefit people?

_____

Landmarks

One natural landmark in the Caribbean attracts hikers and climbers. It is Rio Camuy Caves in Puerto Rico. These caves were carved out by the Camuy River over a million years ago. Cave explorers enjoy the unusual shapes found here below Earth's surface. Would you like to be a cave explorer?

One of the Caribbean's most famous man-made landmarks is the Citadel. This fort was built on top of a mountain in Haiti. It took nearly 15 years and 20,000 workers to build it! One of the oldest man-made landmarks in the Caribbean is Santo Domingo, in the Dominican Republic. Europeans began this community over 500 years ago! You can still visit the historic district of Santo Domingo today.

▲ **Rio Camuy Caves**

▲ **Historic district of Santo Domingo**

> **Think about the Caribbean's climate. What clothes would you pack for a trip to explore Rio Camuy Caves?**
>
> _____
>
> _____

(t)Danita Delimont/Alamy,(b)Pixtal/age fotostock

Lesson **5**

(?) **Essential Question**   How are places unique and different?

_____

_____

_____

_____

Go back to *Show As You Go!* on pages 2–3. ⟪

Analogies show relationships between words.
Complete each analogy with the correct word from the list below.

arid	**phosphate**	**vegetation**	**continent**
tundra	**arable land**	**satellite image**	**climate**

1. *Atlantic* is to *ocean* as *North America* is to _____.

2. *Orange* is to *fruit* as _____ is to *mineral*.

3. _____ is to *desert* as *wet* is to *rain forest*.

4. *Mountain* is to *landform* as *cactus* is to _____.

5. _____ is to *planting* as *ocean* is to *fishing*.

6. *Weather* is to _____ as *sea level* is to *elevation*.

7. _____ is to *Canada* as *plateau* is to *Mexico*.

8. *Portrait* is to *family* as _____ is to *Earth*.

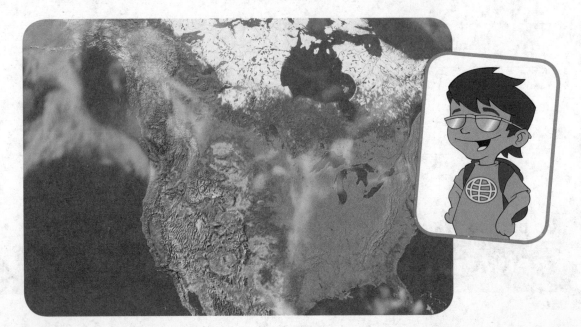

Bill Brooks/Alamy

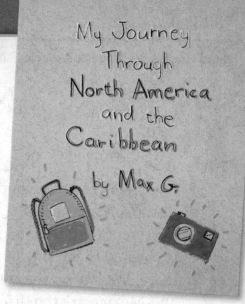

My Journey Through North America and the Caribbean by Max G.

Think about what you have learned about the geography of North America and the Caribbean. You will create a travelogue of the locations in this unit. First, look back at Show As You Go on pages 2 and 3 to review your notes. Then, read the list below to see what should be included in your travelogue. Check off the tasks you have completed.

Your travelogue should include: **Yes, it does!**

a creative title   ☐

at least four entries   ☐

a vocabulary word from each lesson   ☐

two pictures for each entry   ☐

a route map with a map key and compass rose   ☐

Think about the Big Idea

BIG IDEA Location affects how people live.

What did you learn in this unit that helps you understand the BIG IDEA?

_____

_____

_____

_____

Read the article "North America" before answering Numbers 1 through 8.

North America

By Jenny Croft

There are seven continents in the world—North America, South America, Europe, Asia, Australia, Africa, and Antarctica. Of the seven, Antarctica is a continent that does not have any towns or cities where people live because it is covered in ice and snow. All the other continents have many people living there. We live on the continent of North America. Canada, the United States, and Mexico are the three largest countries on the continent.

Canada is the northern-most country on the continent. Much of its northern land is tundra. The southern land is a mixture of mountains, plains, and coastlines. Many people live in cities. Others live in small towns in the country.

Most of the United States is in the middle of North America. Alaska is separated from the rest of the country by Canada. The geography of Alaska is a mix of mountains, tundra, and lush forests filled with trees and wildlife. Hawaii is a group of volcanic islands in the Pacific Ocean. In the continental United States, the geography varies from coastline to mountains to plains to desert. People live in different geographic areas throughout the United States.

Mexico is located in the southern part of North America. It also has a mix of coastlines, deserts, and mountains. It also has many rain forests. Most of the people live in and around cities. Others live in small towns or on farms in the country. Very few people live in the desert.

1 What is the MOST LIKELY reason the author wrote the article "North America"?

Ⓐ to describe the continent of Antarctica

Ⓑ to describe the continent of North America

Ⓒ to describe the continent of the United States

Ⓓ to describe the continent of Mexico

2 Why don't people live on Antarctica?

Ⓕ It is too dark.

Ⓖ There are too many animals.

Ⓗ The temperature is too cold.

Ⓘ The land has too many mountains.

3 Read this sentence from the article.

The geography of Alaska is a mix of mountains, tundra, and lush forests filled with trees and wildlife.

What does the word *lush* mean?

Ⓐ empty

Ⓑ dark

Ⓒ cold

Ⓓ thick

4 How are Canada and Mexico ALIKE?

Ⓕ Very few people live in the tundra.

Ⓖ Some people live in small towns in the country.

Ⓗ Most people live in the mountains.

Ⓘ Very few people live in the desert.

5 With which statement would the author MOST LIKELY agree?

Ⓐ North America has many different types of land.

Ⓑ North America has too many deserts.

Ⓒ Hawaii is the most tropical place to live in North America.

Ⓓ Mexico is the largest country on North America.

6 Where would you find the author's name for this article?

Ⓕ at the end of the article

Ⓖ in the middle of the article

Ⓗ above the title of the article

Ⓘ under the title of the article

7 What is the geography of Alaska?

Ⓐ a mix of plains and tundra

Ⓑ a mix of tundra and forests

Ⓒ a mix of mountains and desert

Ⓓ a mix of desert and plains

8 Which three countries is the author writing about?

Ⓕ North America, Canada, and Mexico

Ⓖ Asia, Antartica, and Africa

Ⓗ Europe, Canada, and the United States

Ⓘ Canada, the United States, and Mexico

2 Celebrating Culture

Jose Fuste Raga/Corbis

BIG IDEA Culture influences the way people live.

Every country has its own culture, or way of life. The culture of the United States is special. It is made up of different customs and traditions brought by the many groups of people who have moved here over the years. In this unit, you will learn about the culture of the United States. You will also compare our culture to the cultures of our neighboring countries. As you read, think about how different cultures influence life in the United States—and your life!

networks

There's More Online!
- Skill Builders
- Vocabulary Flashcards

Show As You Go! Pretend you have just moved to the United States from Canada, Mexico, or the Caribbean. After you read each lesson, compare the culture in your home country to the culture of the United States. You will use your notes to help you complete a project at the end of the unit.

My Home Country

I am from _____. Some of the people who settled

there long ago were _____. In my home country, we

_____

_____

My Life in the United States

Today, I live in the state of _____. It is in the _____

region of the United States. Since moving to the United States, I have learned

_____

_____

_____

_____

Things That are the Same	Things That are Different

Common Core Standards
RI.2 Determine the main idea of a text; recount the key details and explain how they support the main idea.

Summarize the Main Idea and Key Details

The main idea tells what a text passage is about. Often the main idea is in the first sentence of a paragraph. The other sentences have key details that tell more about the main idea. Finding the main idea and key details will help you understand what you are learning. Then you can summarize the passage to explain what it is about.

LEARN IT

- Read the paragraph. Ask, "What is this paragraph about?" See if there is a sentence which states the main idea.

- Look for key details that give more information about the main idea.

- Summarize the paragraph. Sometimes your summary will be the same as the main idea.

> This is the main idea.

There are lots of things to do in the Northeast. If you like the outdoors, you can hike in the mountains or sail along the coast. You can view fine art at many museums in the region. If you love to play sports, go to a park! There, you can find people of all ages playing baseball, soccer, football, or basketball.

> This is a key detail. Underline two other key details.

© Punchstock/BananaStock

56

TRY IT

Use the graphic organizer to write the main idea and key details from the paragraph on page 56. Then complete the sentence.

Main Idea

Key Details

Summary

This paragraph is about _____

_____.

APPLY IT

Read the paragraph below. Circle the main idea. Underline the key details.

There are many different languages spoken throughout the United States. Many people speak only English. Others speak other languages in addition to English. Aside from English, Spanish is the language you hear most often. Other languages spoken in the United States include French Creole, Portuguese, German, and Russian.

What is this paragraph about?

_____

_____

_____

Words to Know

The list below shows some important words you will learn in this unit. Their definitions can be found on the next page. Read the words.

culture (KUL • chuhr)

artifact (AHR • tih • fakt)

diversity (duh • VEHRS • ih • tee)

contribution
(kahn • truh • BYOO • shuhn)

cuisine (kwih • ZEEN)

civilization
(sih • vuh • luh • ZAY • shuhn)

tradition (truh • DIH • shuhn)

heritage (HEHR • uh • tihj)

The Foldable on the next page will help you learn these important words. Follow the steps below to make your Foldable.

Step 1 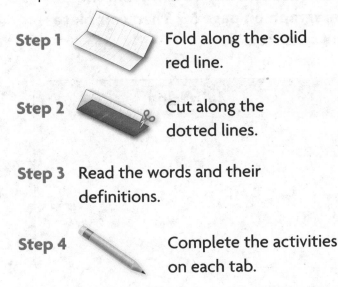 Fold along the solid red line.

Step 2 Cut along the dotted lines.

Step 3 Read the words and their definitions.

Step 4 Complete the activities on each tab.

Step 5 Look at the back of your Foldable. Choose ONE of these activities for each word to help you remember its meaning:

- Draw a picture of the word.

- Write a description of the word.

- Write how the word is related to something you know.

Blend Images/SuperStock

◀ **These musicians play traditional Mexican music.**

	FOLD
Culture is the way of life shared by a group of people.	**Write a sentence using the word *culture*.**
An **artifact** is something that was made or used by people in the past.	**Circle the words that belong with *artifact*.** tool yellow bright painting old hot
Diversity means to have influences from many different cultures.	**Write a sentence using the word *diversity*.**
A **contribution** is the act of giving or doing something.	**Circle two key words in the definition of *contribution*. Write the words here:** _____ _____
Cuisine is a style of cooking.	**Write a synonym for the word *cuisine*.**
A **civilization** is a developed community.	**Write a sentence using the word *civilization*.**
A **tradition** is a way of doing something that has been passed along by families for many years.	**What is one tradition you share with your family?**
Heritage is ways of life handed down from the past.	**Write a sentence using the word *heritage*.**

culture

culture

CUT HERE

artifact

artifact

diversity

diversity

contribution

contribution

cuisine

cuisine

civilization

civilization

tradition

tradition

heritage

heritage

Primary Sources

Artifacts

An artifact is one type of primary source. An artifact is something that was made or used by people in the past. Artifacts can be items such as pots, tools, or art. You can analyze, or study, artifacts to understand how people lived long ago.

In this unit, you will learn about different people who lived in North America and the Caribbean. The artifacts on this page were used by Native Americans. Ask these questions as you study the top artifact.

- **What am I looking at?** This is an arrowhead.

- **What is the object made from?** It is made from stone.

- **How could the object have been used?** It is sharp and pointed. It could be used like a knife to cut things.

- **Why is this artifact important?** The arrowhead shows us how Native Americans lived. They learned to make tools from items in the environment around them.

 Document-Based Questions

Use the bottom artifact to answer the question below.

What is this artifact, and how do you think it was used? Explain your answer.

_____

_____

_____

_____

networks
There's More Online!
● Skill Builders
● Resource Library

All About Culture

(?) Essential Question

How does environment affect culture?
What do you think?

_____

_____

_____

_____

Words To Know

Write what you think each word means on the lines.

culture _____

_____

history _____

_____

agriculture _____

_____

*frame _____

_____

What Is Culture?

What is **culture**, and why is it important? Culture is the way of life of a group of people. It includes things like language, music, sports, clothing, and food. Culture also includes customs. In this unit, you will learn about the cultures of the United States, Canada, Mexico, and the Caribbean.

The United States has many cultures from ethnic groups from all over the world. An ethnic group is a group of people who share the same original culture. When people from different ethnic groups moved here, they brought with them different languages, foods, music, and customs. These different cultures have blended together to create the culture of the United States.

People have their own culture, too. Think about what music you like or how you celebrate holidays with your family. This is part of your culture. As you read, think about how your culture is similar to and different from other cultures.

© Corbis

So, what *is* your culture? Answering the questions below will help you define your culture. You can use this page to help you compare and contrast your culture with other cultures in North America.

How do you and your family celebrate holidays?

_____

_____

What language or languages do you and your family speak at home?

_____

_____

What foods do you eat?

_____

_____

What is your home like?

_____

_____

What types of music do you enjoy?

_____

_____

What do you do for fun?

_____

_____

Native Americans

(tl) Library of Congress, Prints and Photographs Division [LC-USZ62-120023]; (bl) Michael S. Nolan/age fotostock; (br) Ingram Publishing/SuperStock

Reading Skill

Compare and Contrast (Circle) how Native American homes were similar. Underline how they were different.

One way to learn about different cultures is to study the events of the past. This study is called **history**. Let's start by learning about the first people who lived in North America—the Native Americans. They lived in the areas that are now Canada, the United States, Mexico, and the islands of the Caribbean. Native Americans had different ways of life, depending on their environment.

Long ago, people had to use the land, animals, and water around them to help them live. Some Native Americans lived in the icy lands of Alaska and Northern Canada. They fished through the ice for food. They wore clothes made from animal skins to keep warm. Sometimes they even built their houses from snow!

Native Americans who lived along the coasts often lived in small villages. They used the wood from trees to build homes. They fished in the ocean for food. Some used the land around them for **agriculture**, or growing crops and raising animals. Others hunted for food in the forests.

Some Native Americans who lived on the plains were hunters. They were often on the move because they followed the animals they were hunting. Some of their homes looked like tents and were made out of animal skins. The **frames** of their homes could be easily moved.

Native Americans in Florida and the Caribbean

Native Americans also lived in the area that is now Florida and the Caribbean. They fished in the streams, rivers, lakes, and oceans near their homes. They also ate animals and plants that lived near their homes. Like other Native Americans, they built homes and created tools from things they found in the environment. Homes were built out of trees and other plants. Tools and weapons were made from stone and wood.

The pictures on this page show **artifacts** from Native Americans. An artifact is something that was made or used by people in the past. The clay pot held water. The stone arrowhead was a tool used to cut food.

1. Explain how the environment affected Native American life.

_____

_____

_____

2. Imagine someone was studying your culture 500 years from now. Draw a picture of artifacts they would find.

Write a caption for each of the photographs on these pages.

THINK · PAIR · SHARE
How might these artifacts have been used? Discuss your answer with a partner.

European Settlers

As time went on, Europeans began exploring North America and the Caribbean. Soon, immigrants began moving to these areas from other countries.

Spain

The Spanish were the first Europeans to explore North America and the Caribbean. The Dominican Republic became a Spanish colony after Christopher Columbus landed there in 1492. The Spanish also settled in the United States, mainly exploring the Southeast, the Southwest, and Mexico. Signs of Spanish and Mexican influences are seen across the Southwest. For example, Spanish styles are still seen in many buildings in the region.

England

English explorers settled along the mid-Atlantic coast north into Canada. One of their first colonies—Jamestown, Virginia—was built along the banks of the James River. Settlers used the river water for drinking, bathing, and cooking. They also learned from Native Americans how to grow and harvest crops. The English brought many things with them to the United States, including their language. That's one reason we speak English today!

France

The French settled in two main areas of North America. The first was in Canada, along the Saint Lawrence River and in parts of Newfoundland. The other was along the Gulf of Mexico. Many French settlers stayed in the north, but some moved to what is now New Orleans, Louisiana. Here, their lives and customs mixed with those of Native Americans and Africans, who had also moved to the area. Today, some people speak French Creole, which has French, Native American, Spanish, and West African roots.

 Underline examples of Spanish, English, and French influences on the culture of the United States.

United States, Mexico and the Caribbean

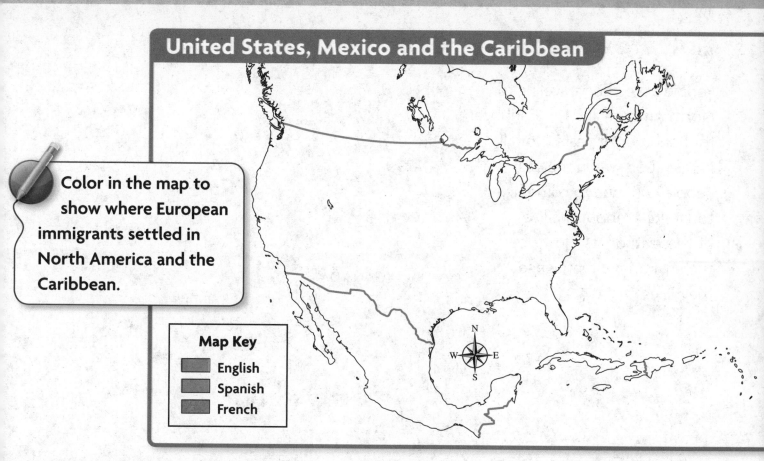

Color in the map to show where European immigrants settled in North America and the Caribbean.

Map Key

- English
- Spanish
- French

Moving West

Most Europeans settled along the east coast and in the Midwest. Over time, more people began to travel farther west across North America. This presented a challenge. What forms of **transportation**, or ways of getting from one place to another, did people use?

Native Americans often traveled by foot to get to new locations. European explorers traveled to North America by boat. In the 1800s, many people used horses or wagons to get to their new homes. In the late 1800s, trains and automobiles were used. Today, many people travel by car or airplane.

DID YOU KNOW?

In the Midwest, a trading post began near Lake Michigan. This trading post became the city of Chicago.

Chart and Graph Skills

Complete the timeline to show what type of transportation you would use today to travel from state to state.

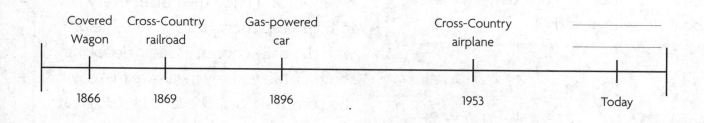

Covered Wagon	Cross-Country railroad	Gas-powered car	Cross-Country airplane	_____
1866	1869	1896	1953	Today

Cultures Today

People have been traveling to North America and the Caribbean for hundreds of years. Not all immigration was in the past. People continue to come here today. Read about the lives of these students. How does the environment influence their lives?

PACIFIC OCEAN

Hudson Bay

CANADA

Vancouver

Ottawa

ATLANTIC OCEAN

Washington, D.C.

UNITED STATES

Tallahassee

BAHAMAS

DOMINICAN REPUBLIC

Saltillo

Gulf of Mexico

CUBA

MEXICO

Kingston

HAITI

PUERTO RICO (U.S.)

Mexico City

JAMAICA

Caribbean Sea

I'm Sidney, and I live in Canada. Some people think that everyone in Canada lives out in the country and plays ice hockey. That's not true! I live in a big city near water and mountains. One reason people live here is because it has the mildest climate in Canada. I can ski in the mountains one day, and take a boat ride the next day!

I'm Rafael, and I live in the Mexican countryside. My family owns a farm. We raise horses and grow corn. My mom and I ride the horses every day to help keep them healthy. I also help with the daily chores, including cooking some of the yummy meals we make with the corn we grow! The land here is great for agriculture.

1. Draw a line from the box to your hometown on the map.

2. Write a biography about your life in your state.

_____

_____

_____

_____

_____

I'm Tia, and I live in Jamaica. My whole world is surrounded by water! I like to go fishing with my parents. I help them make meals with the fresh seafood we catch. Our special recipe has been passed down through my mother's family for many years. I also like to paint the beautiful plants and animals of my island!

BananaStock/PunchStock

Lesson 1

? **Essential Question** How does the environment affect culture?

_____

_____

_____

Go back to *Show As You Go!* on pages 54–55. «

networks   connected.mcgraw-hill.com
● Games ● Assessment

Life in the United States

? Essential Question

How does diversity influence culture?

What do you think?

_____

_____

_____

_____

_____

Words To Know

Write a word that you have seen that looks similar to the words below.

diversity

_____

contribution

_____

*observe

_____

How well do you know your classmates? Find out more about people in your class. Ask questions such as, "What do you like to eat?" "What do you do when you're not in school?" or "What kind of music do you like?" Write the information in the boxes.

Classmate 1 _____

_____

_____

_____

Classmate 2 _____

_____

_____

_____

Classmate 3 _____

_____

_____

_____

Different Cultures, One Country

Read over the information you wrote. Do all of your classmates like the same things? Probably not. That's because we have a lot of **diversity** in the United States. Diversity means to have influences from many different cultures. People across the United States have different interests in music, food, how they spend their free time, and many other things.

Where did this diversity come from? In the last lesson, you learned about the many immigrants who have come to the United States. They brought their cultures with them. These different languages, customs, food, and music contributed to the culture of the United States. A **contribution** is the act of giving or doing something. In this lesson, you will learn about many of the things that make up the culture of the United States.

THINK · PAIR · SHARE
Think about how you would answer the questions you asked your classmates. Share your answers with a partner.

Draw an example of something that has contributed to the culture of the United States.

A family celebrates Thanksgiving in the United States. ▶

Beliefs and Customs

Everywhere you look, you can see how other cultures contribute to American culture. Some customs have been brought to the United States by immigrants. Other customs were created right here. One example of an American custom is to say "hello" and shake hands when you meet someone.

In the United States, people **observe** different holidays based on their beliefs or culture. Some holidays we celebrate include Christmas, Rosh Hashanah, Kwanzaa, and Ramadan. These celebrations each have their own customs. These customs show the diversity of Americans and our respect for one another.

Thanksgiving is a national holiday shared by all Americans. It began long ago, when Native Americans taught European settlers how to grow new crops. The settlers thanked God and the Native Americans for their help by asking them to share a meal. Today, we celebrate by sharing meals with family and friends each November.

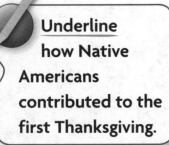

Underline how Native Americans contributed to the first Thanksgiving.

Draw a picture of a custom you have.

Celebrations Across the Country

Different cultures are celebrated in different parts of the country, too. For example, a Winter Carnival is held in Minnesota every year to celebrate the Midwest's cold weather. What other celebrations happen in the United States?

Circle the ethnic groups that have contributed to the different celebrations in the United States. Underline their contributions.

Many African Americans celebrate Kwanzaa throughout the country. One tradition is to light a candle on each night of the celebration.

The Chinese New Year celebration in San Francisco, California, is the largest celebration of Asian culture in North America.

Some people in the Southwest participate in Native American ceremonies such as the Hopi Snake Dance or the Rain Dance of the Zuni.

Many people in the Southwest celebrate the Mexican holiday of Cinco de Mayo. This holiday honors the Mexican army's victory over French soldiers.

Many Irish immigrants settled in the Northeast. Today, people celebrate their Irish roots by attending parades held throughout the region on Saint Patrick's Day.

Mardi Gras celebrations were started in the Southeast by French settlers. Today, people celebrate this carnival with parades, floats, and colorful costumes.

Food and Shelter

What kinds of food do you eat? Fresh fruits and vegetables, corn, wheat, beef, poultry, and seafood are foods found across the United States. Immigrants brought foods with them, too. These foods mixed with traditional American foods to create another part of our culture. Do you like to snack on tortilla chips and salsa? Immigrants from Mexico brought these foods to the United States.

Some regions are known for certain kinds of food. Gumbo is a popular seafood dish in the Southeast. It is a blend of ingredients from French, Spanish, and Native American cultures. Cuban and other Caribbean foods are found in many places throughout the Southeast. A seafood dish known as sushi, originally found in Asian countries, is popular in the Northeast and West. Many foods in the Southwest are a blend of Native American and Mexican influences. And in the Midwest, many foods contain corn, wheat, or soy products grown in the region.

▲ Chips and salsa are a popular Mexican dish.

▲ Sushi rolls

1. **Why do you think Asian food dishes are popular in the Northeast and West?**

   _____

   _____

2. **What types of food do you eat?**

   _____

   _____

3. **What cultures influenced your food?**

   _____

Housing

Our homes are another part of our culture. You've already learned that the types of homes people lived in long ago depended on the environment. The same is true today. Some people live in big cities. These urban areas are crowded and do not have a lot of open space. There are many buildings very close to each other. People usually live in apartments or townhouses.

Other people live in suburbs, which are communities near cities. Suburbs have their own kinds of homes. There, homes are usually farther apart than in a city. People also live in rural areas. Rural areas have many farms and open space. They also have fewer people than the suburbs. Homes may be miles apart from one another. What kind of community and home do you live in?

> **Draw a picture of the type of home you live in.**

Sights and Sounds

Every culture also has its own special music. When people move from one place to another, they bring the music they love with them. Africans who came to the United States, for example, brought their music with them. Jazz, blues, and ragtime are all kinds of music that grew out of African music.

Bluegrass is a type of folk music played on fiddles, banjos, and guitars. It traces its roots to immigrants from Ireland and Scotland who settled in the Appalachian Mountains. The Midwest is also known for its music. Cleveland, Ohio, disc jockey Alan Freed helped promote rock and roll in the 1950s. Detroit, Michigan, is famous for its soul music. Nashville, Tennessee, is the home of country music.

Fun Facts about Music

- Jazz began in New Orleans, Louisiana.
- Hip-hop music began in New York City.
- Country music combines songs from cowboys in the West with folk music from the East.
- Zydeco, a musical style that uses an accordion, comes from the Cajuns of southern Louisiana.
- Rock and roll music began in the South. It combines country, jazz, and African American rhythms.
- Soul music combines African American gospel songs with blues music.

The Rock and Roll Hall of Fame is in Cleveland, Ohio.

What type of music do you listen to the most?

_____

_____

_____

Things to See and Do

Do you love to play sports? Sports are an important part of a culture. Many sports are played throughout the United States. Lacrosse was created by Native Americans hundreds of years ago. It was probably North America's first sport. French settlers in Canada began playing it, too. Ice hockey may have developed from this Native American game. Baseball, soccer, football, and basketball are just some of other types of sports we play.

Where people live also affects what type of activities they do. Many people who live near mountains like to hike. People who live near the ocean often sail boats along the coast. In the Midwest, many people visit museums to see artifacts and fine art. In the West, many people camp and visit national parks. In warmer regions, people can visit theme parks and aquariums year-round.

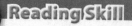

Reading Skill

In the first paragraph, circle the main idea. Underline the key details.

77

Languages and Stories

Another way to learn about a culture is to study its language and stories. Did you know that many English words are based on the German language? English is the most widely spoken language in the United States. But we have many other languages as well! Spanish, French, Haitian Creole, Chinese, and Portuguese are just some examples of the languages people speak. Many of these languages were brought to the United States by immigrants.

You can learn about different cultures by studying poems, legends, and songs, too. Some stories are told to answer questions about people or events from the past. Others teach morals or lessons. No matter what kind of story is told, people can share their culture with others through stories.

The **media** also helps us understand other cultures. Information can travel all over the world through the media. Examples of media are the internet, television, radio, and newspaper. They provide us a nonfiction way to discuss cultures and how others may live.

DID YOU KNOW?
Native Americans used their language to help the United States during World War II. They spoke their language over radios so that enemy soldiers could not understand what was being said.

National Archives and Records Administration [07428]

Put It All Together!

The United States has a very diverse culture. Some characteristics are the same across the country. Others are specific to each region. Complete the chart below with information you learned about each region. This chart will be useful as you read the rest of the unit!

Region of the United States	Notes About the Region's Culture
Southeast	
Northeast	
Midwest	
Southwest	
West	

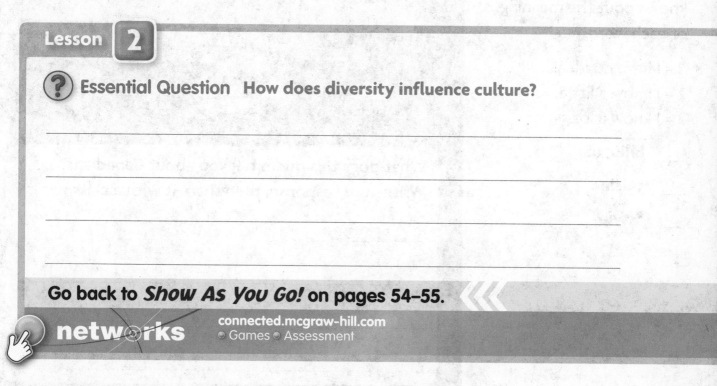

Lesson 2

? **Essential Question** How does diversity influence culture?

_____

_____

_____

_____

Go back to _Show As You Go!_ on pages 54–55. «

? Essential Question

How does diversity influence culture?

What do you think?

_____

_____

_____

_____

_____

Words To Know

Write a number on each line to show how much you know about the meaning of each word.

1 = I have no idea!

2 = I know a little.

3 = I know a lot.

____ **bilingual**

____ **cuisine**

____ ***style**

The people who live in Canada are called Canadians. Just like you, they are proud of their home! Read the poem below.

"My Own Canadian Home"

by E.G. Nelson

Though other skies may be as bright,
And other lands as fair;
Though charms of other **climes**[1] invite
My wandering footsteps there,
Yet there is one, the **peer**[2] of all
Beneath bright heaven's dome;
Of thee I sing, O happy land,
My own Canadian home!

[1] **climes** climate
[2] **peer** friend

What does this poem tell you about Canadians? Write your response, then share it with a classmate.

_____

_____

_____

_____

Who Are Canadians?

There are around 33 million people living in Canada. Native Americans make up over a million of these people. Native Americans lived in Canada for thousands of years before European settlers arrived. Some lived in coastal fishing villages. Others were hunters and gatherers. Still others created permanent settlements. Some Native Americans even lived in the icy Arctic. Today, Native Americans still live throughout the country.

But Native Americans aren't the only people living in Canada. Like the United States, Canada is home to people from Asia, Africa, Latin America, and many other parts of the world. Most of Canada's immigrants came from Europe. The French settled Canada in the 1600s. For over 200 years, they ruled much of the eastern part of the country. Later, the British gained control of Canada. Because of these influences from France and England, many Canadians today are **bilingual**. That means they speak two languages.

A community on the French River in Prince Edward Island ▼

How are the languages spoken in Canada similar to those spoken in the Southeast United States?

_____

_____

Living in Canada

Many immigrants have moved to Canada over the years. They brought with them many of the customs of their homelands. These different customs are a part of Canada's culture. Let's read about life in some of Canada's major cities.

Quebec

The city of Quebec was the first French settlement in Canada. It was built on the banks of the Saint Lawrence River. More than 500,000 people live in Quebec today. There are many French, African, and Asian **cuisines**, or styles of cooking, found throughout the city. One of Quebec's biggest attractions is the Winter Carnival. Visitors come to the city to see large snow sculptures and to visit the ice palace—a giant building made entirely of ice!

Montreal

Montreal is the second-largest city in Canada. It has the largest population of French-speaking Canadians. French culture is seen and heard throughout the city. Many festivals are held throughout the year to celebrate its French roots. The city is a major center of culture, education, and business as well.

Toronto

Toronto has the largest population of all Canadian cities. More than half of the city's residents were born in other countries. Some of this diversity is seen in Toronto's food. Many different cuisines are found in restaurants throughout the city. Toronto is also home to many businesses, theaters, and museums. It also has the CN Tower. This tower is 1,815 feet tall, which makes it the tallest free-standing structure in the Western Hemisphere!

> **How is Toronto similar to cities in the United States?**
>
> _____
>
> _____

Ottawa

Ottawa is the capital of Canada. It is located in the province of Ontario, between Toronto and Montreal. One unique feature of the city is the Rideau Canal. This man-made waterway connects the city to Lake Ontario. During the winter, a 5-mile stretch of the canal becomes one of the longest skating rinks in the world!

Vancouver

Vancouver is a large city located on Canada's west coast. About one-third of the people living in Vancouver were born in other countries, including Asia and Europe. One reason people live here is because it has the mildest climate in Canada. This allows for outdoor activities year-round. People can ski, play soccer, and go kayaking all in the same day!

How does the United States compare to Canada? Choose one U.S. region and compare it to Canada in the diagram below.

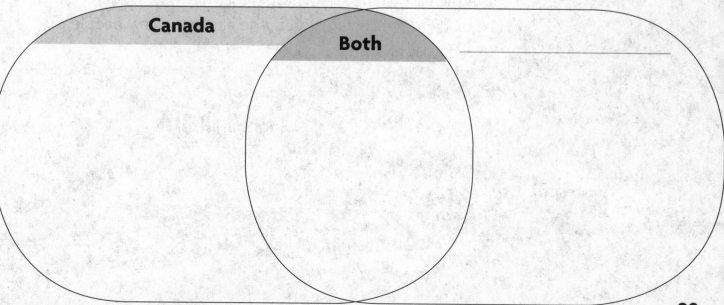

Canada   Both   _____

Things to Do in Canada

There is much to see and do in Canada. Citizens and visitors can attend plays, museums, sporting events, and celebrations throughout the country, all year round.

Sports

During the winter, children enjoy ice skating, skiing, and ice hockey—the most popular sport in Canada. During the summer, Canadians spend much of their time outdoors. Lacrosse, water sports, and fishing are popular activities. They also play games such as baseball and soccer.

Circle the parts of Canadian culture that are similar to the culture of the Northeast United States.

Traveling Through Canada

A train travels through Alberta, Canada ▼

Like the United States, Canada is a big country. How do people get to different places? Long ago, boats and canoes were the only way people and goods could travel across Canada's lakes and rivers. Today, railroads and highways connect cities and towns. The Trans-Canada Highway stretches across the country from the east to the west coast. Other highways connect cities in Canada to the United States. And airplanes allow people to travel quickly around the country and the world.

Cuisine, Holidays, and the Arts

Since Canada's people are very diverse, so is the food! The **style** of traditional Canadian food is very similar to American food. Meat, seafood, fruits, vegetables, and grains are important ingredients. Cuisines from Europe, the Caribbean, and Asia are also found throughout the country. Canadians also enjoy many Native American foods, such as pan-fried bread.

Canadians celebrate holidays, too. They celebrate Thanksgiving, much like we do in America. However, their celebration is in October, not November! They also celebrate Canada Day on July 1. This is a celebration of the day Canada became a country in 1867.

Canadians also enjoy theater and the arts. People can see plays at Ontario's Stratford Shakespeare Festival. Many movies and television shows are filmed in cities such as Toronto and Vancouver. Canadian art reflects both European and Native American influences. Many artists are inspired by the landscape of the country.

> **Reading Skill**
> **Main Idea and Key Details**
> Underline the key details that explain what types of food are found in Canada.

Lesson 3

? Essential Question   How does diversity influence culture?

_____

_____

_____

_____

_____

Go back to *Show As You Go!* on pages 54–55. «

Life in Mexico

How does diversity influence culture?
What do you think?

_____

_____

_____

Words To Know

Find the definition for each word. Then write other words that come to mind when you think of each word.

civilization _____

_____

generation _____

_____

tradition _____

_____

***compare** _____

_____

Did you know that rocks can be used as a calendar? The early peoples of Mexico did! The Maya and the Aztec were two of the first **civilizations,** *or developed communities, who lived in Mexico. The Maya built a pyramid out of rocks to track the seasons. The Aztec used a calendar stone. Even though these civilizations counted 365 days in a year just like we do, other parts were measured differently. There were 18 months in a year. Each month had approximately 20 days. These calendars were used to help plan for farming and predict the weather.*

How do you use calendars?

_____

_____

Author's Image/PunchStock

Hi, it's Emilio again! I went to Mexico last summer to visit my grandparents. I learned a lot while I was there!

The People of Mexico

The Maya and the Aztec did more than just use rocks to keep track of time. The Maya built houses, temples, and pyramids in southern Mexico. Mayan people still live in southern Mexico today. The Aztec founded many cities and towns. Their capital, Tenochtitlán, was built in the middle of a beautiful lake. This is where Mexico City is located today.

These civilizations lived alone until Spanish explorers came to the area that is now Mexico in the 1500s. The Spanish took control of the land and ruled for almost 300 years. As Spanish colonists moved there, they brought many things with them. Horses, donkeys, and oxen were new to Mexico. The Spanish also brought the wheel to Mexico. All of these helped with farming, especially with an important new crop—sugarcane. The Spanish also brought their language to the native people of Mexico. Today most people in Mexico still speak Spanish. In fact, it is the largest Spanish-speaking country in the world.

Demetrio Carrasco/Dorling Kindersley/Getty Images

Underline the ways in which the Spanish influenced Mexico.

Life Around the Country

Some people in Mexico still live in small villages. Most people live in cities and large towns. A lot of people live in Mexico City, the country's capital. More people live in this urban area than in any other Mexican city. Some people in Mexico City are immigrants. They moved from countries in Europe, Asia, and the Middle East. Because so many people live and work in this city, it's really crowded and has a lot of traffic. But it also has a lot of great places to visit, like museums and theaters. There are a lot of businesses and universities, too.

Did you know that Mexico City is one of the largest cities in the world? More than 20 million people live there!

1. How is life in Mexico City similar to life in the Southeast United States? _____

_____

_____

_____

2. What region of the United States do you think is most like Mexico? Why? _____

_____

_____

People live in other parts of the country, too. The people who live in the Valley of Mexico spend a lot of time outdoors because of the mild weather. People who live in the rain forest get their food from plants, and by hunting and fishing. They work hard to both enjoy and protect the resources of the rain forest. Fewer people live in Mexico's desert areas because it is hard to work and live there. There isn't enough water to grow crops, so farmers in desert villages and towns use pipes or ditches to bring in water from other areas.

▲ Emilio's family made dinner to celebrate his visit.

Family

No matter where people live, family is very important in Mexico. Often, many **generations** live together or near each other. A generation is a group of people born and living around the same time. By living near each other, many generations of a family are able to spend time together and help each other. They also share stories and **traditions**. A tradition is a way of doing something that has been passed along by families for many years. Some traditions include celebrating holidays and cooking special meals. How does family life in Mexico **compare** to your family life?

Draw a picture of a tradition you share with your family.

The Culture of Mexico

The people of Mexico have many celebrations, too! One of the country's most important holidays is Independence Day. Every year on September 16, Mexicans celebrate gaining their independence from Spain. As in the United States, Mexicans also celebrate Cinco de Mayo. This holiday celebrates Mexico's victory over French invaders. Throughout the country, people participate in parades to honor the day.

An important part of any culture is the food. Have you ever eaten a tortilla? It is flat, thin bread made of corn or flour. Tortillas and other corn products are eaten daily in Mexico. Corn, beans, rice, and squash are foods found in many Mexican dishes. Vegetables such as avocados, tomatoes, and potatoes are other ingredients commonly used in Mexican cuisine.

Music is also a part of Mexico's culture. Some musicians play songs on violins, guitars, and other instruments. Others play a type of music called *cumbia*. This music has Caribbean influences. It mixes flutes, drums, and maracas.

A mariachi band is a group of musicians who play violins, guitars, and horns. ▼

What parts of Mexican culture do you see in the United States today?

_____

_____

_____

_____

The Arts and Sports

Just like the United States, the arts and sports are a large part of the Mexico's culture. Many cities have colorful wall paintings called murals. Some murals were influenced by the Aztec and Mayan civilizations. Mexican ballet and theater groups perform throughout the country and around the world.

Sports are important in Mexico as well. *Fútbol* is the most popular sport in Mexico. We call it "soccer" here in the United States. Children and adults play *fútbol* in backyards, at school, and in large stadiums. Baseball is another popular sport. Do you play any of these sports?

Dave Moyer

How are Mexico and the United States similar?

_____

_____

_____

During celebrations, some people wear large hats called sombreros. The hats help people stay cool by keeping the sun off of their faces.

Lesson 4

? **Essential Question** **How does diversity influence culture?**

_____

_____

_____

_____

Go back to *Show As You Go!* on pages 54–55.

Life in the Caribbean

? Essential Question

How does diversity influence culture?
What do you think?

_____

_____

_____

_____

Words To Know

Find the definition for each word and write a synonym on the line. A synonym is a word that has the same or almost the same meaning.

heritage

_____

*include

_____

recreation

_____

The People of the Caribbean

Almost 40 million people live in the Caribbean. Many of these people are a mix of European, African, Native American, and Asian **heritage**. Heritage is something handed down from the past, such as language or culture. Over the centuries, these heritages have blended together throughout the Caribbean.

The native people who lived in the Caribbean were the Taíno. Later, much of the Caribbean was settled by the French and Spanish. Many Africans were brought to the islands as enslaved people to work for the settlers. Eventually, they were freed and continued to live on the islands. Over the years, Africans have added their traditions to the food, music, and arts of the region.

The Spanish, English, French, and Dutch founded colonies on many of the islands of the Caribbean. These colonies **include** Santo Domingo, the first permanent European settlement in the Caribbean. Many Asians also live in the Caribbean. Most came during the 1800s to work on sugarcane farms. They stayed and eventually formed their own communities.

In some Caribbean countries, people developed their own language. They combined parts of different languages from their home countries. One example is Haitian Creole, which is spoken in Haiti. It has French words but uses grammar from African languages. Other Creole languages in the Caribbean are based on English, Spanish, and Dutch. English and French are spoken throughout the whole region.

DID YOU KNOW?
Haiti became the first colony in the region to gain independence from France.

1. **Underline** the cultures that influenced life in the Caribbean.

2. How are languages spoken in the Caribbean similar to languages spoken in the Southeast United States?

_____

_____

Nassau, Bahamas ▼

Cuba

Cuba has the largest population in the Caribbean—about 12 million people. Many of the people are of African, European, and Asian heritage. Cuba was ruled by Spain until 1898. Spanish influences can still be seen and heard throughout the country. For example, most people speak Spanish. Today, the government controls much of the country and the people. Many people have moved to other countries—including the United States—to find freedom.

Jamaica

About 3 million people live in Jamaica. Most of the people are of African heritage, but European and American influences can also be seen around the country. Jamaica was first a Spanish colony. Then it became an English colony. English is the official language, but Spanish and other languages are also spoken. Reggae, a style of dance music that is popular in Jamaica, was influenced by blues music from the Southeast United States.

Dominican Republic

The Dominican Republic is where Christopher Columbus first landed in 1492. It later became a Spanish colony. Most of the people who live there today speak Spanish. Seafood, beans, rice, meat, vegetables, and plantains (a type of banana) are main ingredients in their food. Pottery making and weaving are popular art forms in the Dominican Republic.

Circle the American influences on Caribbean cultures.

Bahamas

The Bahamas is influenced by native, African, and English cultures. It was first settled by English colonists looking for religious freedom. Africans were brought as enslaved people to work on cotton farms. Asian and Hispanic immigrants also live in the Bahamas. A lot of what the people of the Bahamas eat comes from the sea that surrounds them. African rhythms, Caribbean calypso, and English folk songs create a style of music that is unique to the Bahamas.

Puerto Rico

Almost 4 million people live in Puerto Rico. Many live in and around San Juan, the capital. European, African, Hispanic, and American heritages influence life in Puerto Rico. One unique characteristic of Puerto Rico is that it is a commonwealth of the United States. This means that Puerto Ricans are American citizens. They can travel between Puerto Rico and the United States just as easily as you can travel from your state to another state in the United States.

Underline why Puerto Rico is similar to the United States.

Haiti

Haiti is the first nation in the history of the world to be founded by formerly enslaved people. It declared its independence from France in 1804. Today, there are more than 9 million people living in Haiti. Most speak Haitian Creole or French. The food is influenced by the French, with many breads, cheeses, and desserts. Fresh fruit and vegetables are also eaten daily in Haiti. The country is still recovering from a huge earthquake that hit in 2010.

Caribbean Culture

The Caribbean's mild climate makes it a popular spot for **recreation**, or relaxing or playing for fun. Many people from all over the world take trips to the Caribbean every year. They can sail a boat, swim in the ocean, and take hikes around the different islands. These visitors, called tourists, are important to the people of the islands. Many people of the Caribbean earn a living while they share their culture with the tourists.

Holidays and celebrations are an important part of Caribbean culture. Across the Caribbean, a festival known as Carnival is celebrated in the winter months. People wear bright costumes and participate in street parades with colorful floats and different kinds of music. In Puerto Rico, the Merengue Festival is one of the region's most popular Latin music festivals. The Dominican Republic celebrates its Independence Day in February, while the Bahamas celebrates its in July.

> Underline how African culture influences the Caribbean.

Many Caribbean music styles are based on African music and rhythms. These styles also use drums. The steel drum is an instrument unique to the Caribbean. It used to be made out of empty steel oil containers. Today the drums play a wide range of sounds.

How is the Caribbean similar to the Southeast United States?

_____

_____

_____

(tl)Jose Fuste Raga/Corbis; (bl) Photodisc/C Squared Studios/Getty Images

The Caribbean also has unique food with many different influences. When people came to the area from Africa, they tried to recreate the foods of their homes. They had to swap out ingredients and spices for what they could find around them. This resulted in African recipes with Caribbean ingredients!

Like the United States, sports are popular in the Caribbean. Several countries have their own baseball leagues. Many players have left the region to play for professional teams in the United States. Dominoes and soccer are other games played throughout the Caribbean.

▲ People playing dominoes in the Caribbean

What sports are the same in the Caribbean and the United States?

_____

_____

Lesson 5

? **Essential Question** How does diversity influence culture?

_____

_____

_____

_____

_____

_____

Go back to *Show as You Go!* on pages 54–55. ≪

networks   connected.mcgraw-hill.com
● Games ● Assessment

Jeremy Horner/CORBIS

In each circle, give an example of how each group
has contributed to the culture of the United States.

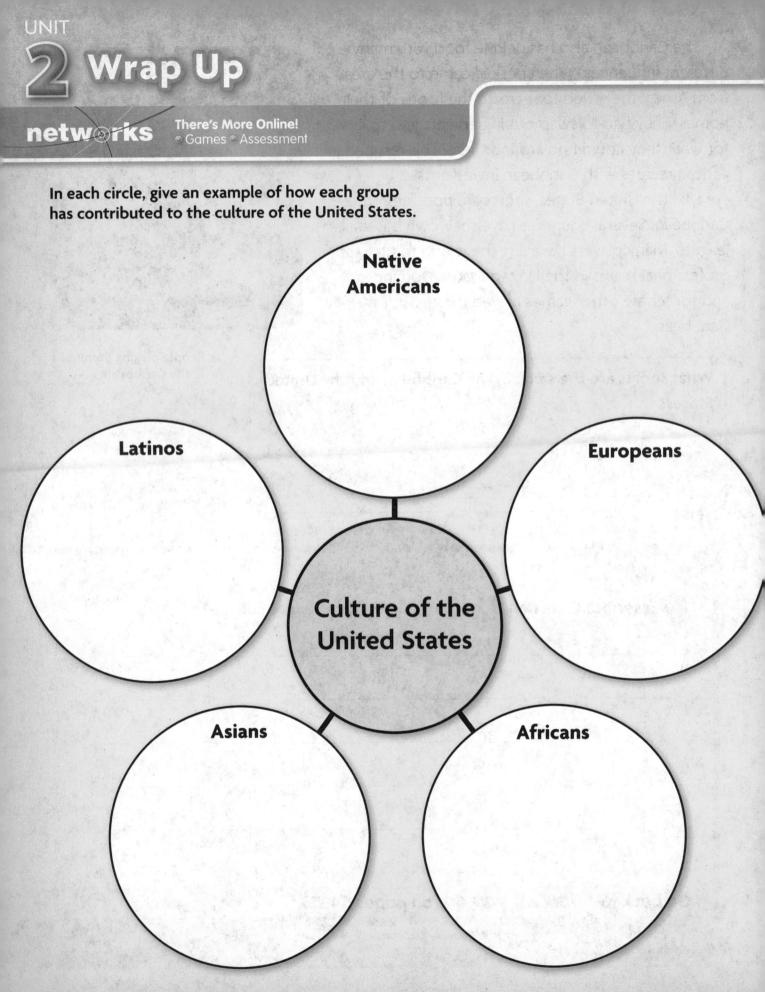

Native
Americans

Latinos

Europeans

Culture of the
United States

Asians

Africans

BIG IDEA

Unit Project

Now it's time to share your story! Use the information from the unit to write and share a story about the cultures you have learned about. Use pages 54 and 55 to help you get started. Read the list below to see what should be included in your story. As you work, check off each task.

Your story should...   **Yes, it does!**

tell what country you are from and explain its culture.   ☐

tell what region of the United States you moved to and
explain its culture.   ☐

compare and contrast your home country with your new home.   ☐

give two examples of how you could contribute to the culture
of your new home   ☐

present information logically and completely.   ☐

Think about the Big Idea

BIG IDEA Culture influences the way people live.

What have you learned about how culture influences the way people live?

_____

_____

_____

_____

99

Read the article "What is Cultural Geography?" before answering Numbers 1 through 8.

What is Cultural Geography?

by Aiden Smith

Why do some people listen to country music and other people listen to rock and roll? Why do some cultures think eating bugs is a delicacy, when others think it's gross? These are the types of questions that people who study cultural geography try to answer.

What is cultural geography? It is the study of how culture begins and changes as people move around the world. It is sometimes called "human geography." Some of the most important parts of cultural geography are art, music, language, and religion. How are physical geography and cultural geography different? Physical geography studies the land. Cultural geography studies how people are affected by the land.

Where people live has an effect on how they live. For example, the earliest civilizations were found near rivers. Rivers provided water for crops, for drinking, and for transportation. Today people who live near the rivers might catch fish and build ships for trade. The environment has changed how people live. People in these areas no longer use the water like they used to. Instead, they have figured out how to make their environment work for them. This has changed their lifestyle and their culture.

1 What is the MOST LIKELY reason the author wrote the article "What Is Cultural Geography?"

Ⓐ to explain the differences between physical geography and cultural geography

Ⓑ to define cultural geography

Ⓒ to define physical geography

Ⓓ to explain the similarities between physical geography and cultural geography

2 With which statement would the author MOST LIKELY agree?

Ⓕ People are not affected by their environments.

Ⓖ Everyone needs water to live.

Ⓗ The study of people is more important than the study of land.

Ⓘ Physical geography is connected to cultural geography.

3 Read this sentence from the article.

"Why do some cultures think eating bugs is a delicacy, when others think it's gross?"

If the word "gross" means *disgusting*, what does the word "delicacy" mean?

Ⓐ pleasure

Ⓑ choice

Ⓒ variety

Ⓓ horrible

4 How is cultural geography SIMILAR to physical geography?

Ⓕ They both study people.

Ⓖ They both study money.

Ⓗ They both study land.

Ⓘ They both study government.

5 Which of the following is studied in cultural geography?

Ⓐ music

Ⓑ rocks

Ⓒ stars

Ⓓ currency

6 Which of the following is a type of question that MIGHT be answered by studying culture?

Ⓕ When is your birthday?

Ⓖ What do you eat?

Ⓗ How old are you?

Ⓘ Are you a boy or a girl?

7 What is another term for "cultural geography"?

Ⓐ physical geography

Ⓑ environmental geography

Ⓒ animal geography

Ⓓ human geography

8 Why did early civilizations settle near water?

Ⓕ Water built ships for people to sail in.

Ⓖ Water provided a place for people to sleep.

Ⓗ Water was used for drinking and cooking.

Ⓘ Water provided a place to grow crops.

BIG IDEA Economics affects people.

You may not notice it, but economics affects us every day. Economics is the way people use money, goods, and services. How do we get the goods and services we want? Long ago people made or grew most of the things they needed. They also traded for things they wanted. Today we find most of our goods and services in stores or on the Internet. Then we buy them with money. In this unit, you will learn about how economics affects people. As you read, think about how economics affects you, too!

After Lesson 1
Circle in green the part of the advertisement that shows the item available for exchange.

After Lesson 2
Circle in yellow the part of the advertisement that shows a resource.

After Lesson 3
Circle in blue the part of the advertisement that shows the item that is scarce.

After Lesson 4
Circle in red the part of the advertisement that shows that currency is accepted.

networks

There's More Online!
- Skill Builders
- Vocabulary Flashcards

Show As You Go! Use the advertisement below to complete the activities on page 102. You can color in the advertisement, too! You will use these pages to help you complete a project at the end of the unit.

Fold page here.

Reading Skill

Common Core Standards
RI.9 Compare and contrast the most important points and key details presented in two texts on the same topic.

Compare and Contrast Texts

When you compare and contrast texts, you can learn more about a topic. To compare means to see how things are alike. To contrast means to see how things are different. Sometimes people have different opinions on the same topic. Other times, the same information is presented in different ways.

> Both texts are about the new camera. This is how they are alike.

> This sentence shows how the texts are different. Underline another sentence that explains how things are different.

(LEARN IT

To compare and contrast texts:

- **Look for ways the texts are alike. What information is the same?**

- **Look for ways the texts are different. What information is not the same?**

Product review: The new Camera Shot 4000 is one of the best products on the market. It takes crisp, clear photographs every time you use it. The settings menu is easy to use, and the memory card stores up to 300 images. This is a great camera for everyone, even beginners!

Blog entry: I just bought the Camera Shot 4000. I had a hard time figuring out which setting to use. I also couldn't get the flash to work. My pictures turned out okay. Maybe I need to learn more about taking pictures before I use the camera again.

© Masterfile (Royalty-Free Division)

A graphic organizer will help you to compare and contrast
texts. Fill in the chart below with the similarities and
differences from the paragraphs on page 104.

Similarities	Differences

APPLY IT

Read the paragraphs below. Circle the items that are alike.
Underline the items that are different. Then answer the questions.

Web site: Farms in the United States
produce a lot of food. Most farms grow
crops or raise animals. Farms can have
fields of crops, orchards of fruit, or land
where animals graze. This food is sent
to people around the world. Are there
farms near you?

Newspaper: The cold weather has
affected many of the south's farms.
Many plants, including oranges, have
been covered with frost. The price
of oranges in the United States has
gone up. Orange shipments were also
reduced due to the losses.

How are these two texts similar?

_____

_____

_____

How are these two texts different?

_____

_____

_____

_____

Words to Know

The list below shows some important words you will learn in this unit. Their definitions can be found on the next page. Read the words.

budget (buh • jit)

buyer (BY • uhr)

currency (KUR • ehnt • see)

demand (dih • MAHND)

economics (eh • kuh • NAH • miks)

exchange (ehks • CHAYNJ)

opportunity cost (opur • tu • nity • kuhst)

seller (SEH • luhr)

supply (suh • PLIH)

scarcity (SKEHR • suh • tee)

FOLDABLES®

The Foldable on the next page will help you learn these important words. Follow the steps below to make your Foldable.

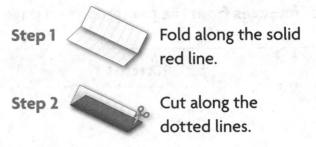

Step 1 Fold along the solid red line.

Step 2 Cut along the dotted lines.

Step 3 Read the words and their definitions.

Step 4 Complete the activities on each tab.

Step 5 Look at the back of your Foldable. Choose ONE of these activities for each word to help you remember its meaning:

- Draw a picture of what the word means.

- Write a description of the word in your own words.

- Write how the word is related to something you know.

William Ryall 2010

Economics is the study of how people use money, goods, and services.	Write a sentence using the word *economics*.
A **buyer** is a person who gives money or trades items for things he or she wants or needs.	Circle the words that belong with the word *buyer*. sells gives goods buys symbol money
A **seller** is a person who takes money or other items in exchange for things he or she wants or needs.	Write a sentence using the word *seller*.
Exchange means to trade or give up one item for another item	Write a synonym for the word *exchange*.
Demand is the number of people who want or need something	Write a sentence using the word *demand*.
Supply is the amount of something that is available.	Circle two key words in the definition of *supply*. Write the words here: _____ _____
Scarcity is when something is difficult to get or find.	What is one thing you want or need that is affected by scarcity?
Currency is a country's system of money.	Write two words that are examples of *currency*. _____ _____

economics

buyer

seller

exchange

demand

supply

scarcity

currency

economics

buyer

seller

exchange

demand

supply

scarcity

currency

CUT HERE

Secondary Sources

Images

Secondary sources analyze primary sources to help us better understand people, places, or events. Paintings, biographies, and magazine articles are examples of secondary sources. We use them to learn more about our past.

Images such as paintings are a type of secondary source. These images tell us about events which happened in the past. Paintings are usually a secondary source because they are generally made after an event is over. They are also usually created by someone who wasn't at the event.

DBQ Document-Based Questions

Use the painting to answer the questions below.

1. Why is this painting a secondary source?

_____

_____

2. What does this painting tell you about our country's history?

_____

_____

Secondary Source

This painting shows the authors of the Declaration of Independence presenting the document to the Continental Congress. The painting is a secondary source because it was made 41 years after the event. Today the painting hangs in the U.S. Capitol. It is also on the back of the two-dollar bill.

networks
There's More Online!
● Skill Builders
● Resource Library

Buyers and Sellers

? Essential Question

How do people interact?
What do you think?

_____

_____

_____

_____

_____

_____

Words To Know

Write a number on each line to show how much you know about the meaning of each word.

1 = I have no idea!
2 = I know a little.
3 = I know a lot.

____ **economics**

____ ***consider**

____ **buyer**

____ **seller**

____ **exchange**

____ **opportunity cost**

What does your family do when they need groceries? They probably go to the grocery store. What about if you want a new video game? Do you go to a store, or do you shop online? Today, we have many options to get what we need and want. Where do you do most of your shopping?

_____

_____

1. Imagine you owned a store. What would you sell?

_____

_____

_____

2. Where would you get the items to sell in your

store? _____

_____

_____

What Is Economics?

Economics is the study of how people use money, goods, and services. Why is it important to learn about economics? Because it affects you every day! **Consider** the things you will use today. Do you picture clothes, food, books, and computers? These items probably come from stores in your community. These stores are part of the community's economy. They are there to provide you and your neighbors with the things you want and need.

In the United States, people work together to make goods and provide services. In this lesson, you will learn about the people who buy and sell the goods you use every day. You will also learn how they work together to get people the things they want and need.

Reading Skill
Text Features
Circle the photo caption on this page. Underline the header on this page.

People shop at stores to buy the things they want and need. ▼

List three things you can buy from stores in your community.

1. _____

2. _____

3. _____

MANAGING MONEY

People plan how to spend their money by deciding what they need and want. To help them make smart money choices, people often make a **budget**. A budget is a plan for using money. It helps people make personal economic decisions for the present and future.

Making a budge involves making decisions. It often means comparing the cost of something with the benefit of having it. A benefit is something that is good or helpful. For example, the television movie channel costs extra money each month. Your family loves to watch movies. The service would be a benefit, so your family has to decide if the cost is worth the benefit. If they want the special movie channel enough, they might have to decide to give up something else to have it!

Giving something up when you choose one thing instead of another is called **opportunity cost**. When choosing the movie channel, the family might choose to give up eating out for dinner every Friday. Eating out would be their opportunity cost.

Why do people need to make a budget?

_____

_____

▼ Budgets help families decide how to spend their money. Groceries are part of this family's budget.

Family Budget

Income (per month)	Expenses	
Mom + Dad $7,800.00	Food	$250.00
	Electricity	$150.00
	Phone	$85.00
	Clothes	$500.00
	Emergencies	$1,500.00

Who Are Buyers and Sellers?

What is a Buyer?

This is Aaron. He's a **buyer**. That means he buys goods and services from other people. Goods are items such as food, books, or video games. A service is something useful that people do for others. When Aaron gets his hair cut or goes to the doctor, he is buying a service.

Where do buyers get goods and services? Everywhere! They buy them at the corner market, in big superstores, and even on the Internet. Buyers use money to pay for the goods and services they want.

What Is a Seller?

Who sells the items buyers want? People like Mrs. Mann, who is a **seller**. A seller is someone who sells goods and services to other people. Mrs. Mann owns a store. That's where she sells most of her products. She also sells them on the Internet. But sellers can be anywhere! People don't just sell goods, either. They also sell services. Sometimes sellers **exchange** goods for other items. To exchange means to swap or give up one item for another item. But sellers usually exchange goods or services for money.

Reading Skill
Meaning of Unknown Words

Underline the text clues that help you understand what the word *useful* means.

Draw a picture of something you would like to buy.

113

Mr. Smith owns a farm. He and his family grow apples to sell to other people at the farmers' market. Mr. Smith is a seller and a producer of apples.

Mr. Smith needs help to run his farm. He buys services from people who pick the apples, put them in boxes, and load them onto trucks. He also buys goods such as ladders, trucks, and boxes. Mr. Smith is also a buyer!

Buyers and Sellers

THINK • PAIR • SHARE
Think back to the store you imagined owning. In this store, are you a buyer, a seller, or both? Discuss your answer with a partner.

Let's take a closer look at how buyers and sellers interact, or work together. Look at the pictures on these pages. Mr. Smith runs a farm that grows, or produces, apples. On his farm, he interacts with sellers to buy ladders, trucks, and boxes. At the market, he sells apples to buyers. He interacts with buyers to exchange his goods for their money. Later, at a music store, Mr. Smith interacts with Mr. Timmons. Mr. Timmons is a seller, and he sells a guitar to Mr. Smith.

So we can see that Mr. Smith is both a buyer and a seller. When Mr. Smith is at the farmers' market, he is a seller and interacts with buyers. When he buys items for his farm or a guitar for his son, he is a buyer and interacts with a seller.

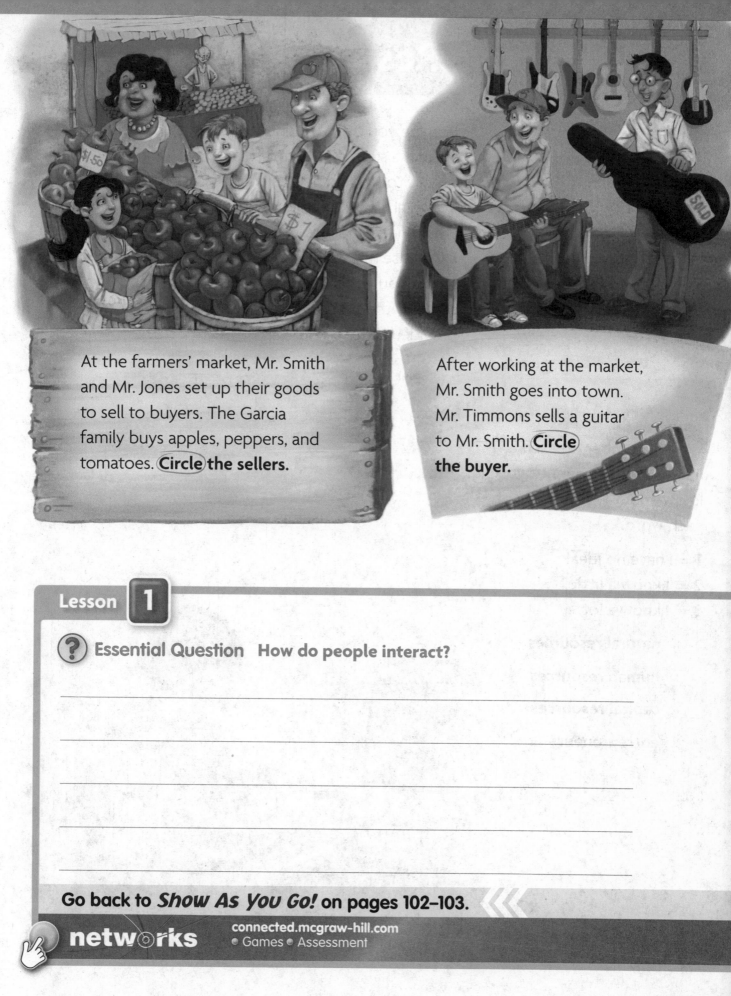

At the farmers' market, Mr. Smith and Mr. Jones set up their goods to sell to buyers. The Garcia family buys apples, peppers, and tomatoes. **Circle** the sellers.

After working at the market, Mr. Smith goes into town. Mr. Timmons sells a guitar to Mr. Smith. **Circle** the buyer.

Lesson 1

? Essential Question How do people interact?

_____

_____

_____

_____

_____

Go back to _Show As You Go!_ on pages 102–103.

networks   connected.mcgraw-hill.com
● Games ● Assessment

Productive Resources

Ryan McVay/Getty Images

? Essential Question

Why are resources important?
What do you think?

_____

_____

_____

_____

Words To Know

Write a number on each line to show how much you know about the meaning of each word.

1 = I have no idea!
2 = I know a little.
3 = I know a lot.

____ **natural resources**

____ **human resources**

____ **capital resources**

____ **entrepreneur**

Imagine you own a business. What would you need to make it a success? You might need a building for your office. You would need electricity and running water. You might need people to help you run the business. You would need supplies, such as desks, chairs, and computers. What else might you need to run your business? Where would you get all these items? Read on to learn about some of the things people use to make goods and provide services.

Natural Resources

An important part of a community's economy is its resources. All economies have three types of resources— natural resources, human resources, and capital resources.

Natural resources are materials found in nature that are useful or necessary to life. Natural resources include water, sunlight, minerals, plants, animals, and soil. They also include places such as lakes and forests.

Some natural resources are used in their natural form. For example, water can be used for drinking, cooking, and washing. Sunlight provides us light and allows plants to grow. Other natural resources must be changed into another form in order to be used. For example, trees are cut down into large pieces called lumber. The lumber can then be used to build houses or furniture. Look around your neighborhood. What natural resources do you see?

▲ **A miner holds a silver nugget**

Joe Belanger/Alamy

What are different ways you use natural resources in your daily life?

_____

_____

_____

_____

_____

Human Resources

Businesses use natural resources to make things people will buy. Businesses also use **human resources** to get work done. Human resources are the people who work for a business. People who run or own a business are called employers. People who work for a business are called employees. Both employers and employees are human resources. Human resources are needed to make goods, to provide services, and to do other kinds of work.

On a farm, the human resources are the people who plant and pick the crops, feed the animals, drive the machines, and sell the crops. In a school, the human resources are teachers, principals, and office staff. In a grocery store, the human resources are the cashiers and the workers who stock the shelves.

▼ Teachers, construction workers, and mail carriers are all human resources.

Hard at Work

Human resources include people who do physical labor and people who do mental labor. Physical labor is work that uses the strength of the body. Mowing lawns and paving roads are examples of physical work. Mental labor is work that uses the mind. Lawyers, doctors, teachers, and writers do mental work. What kinds of work do the people in your family do?

What is the difference between physical and mental work?

_____

_____

_____

_____

Capital Resources

Most people use tools and machines to get their work done. The tools and machines that they use are examples of capital resources. **Capital resources** are goods produced and used to make other goods. Capital resources are also called capital goods.

There are many examples of capital resources all around us. Computers are common capital resources that help people do all kinds of work. Teachers use books as tools to help them teach, so books are capital resources too. Artists use paints and paintbrushes, and cooks use pots, pans, and ovens. All of these tools are capital resources. What kinds of capital resources do you use in your day-to-day life?

How are capital resources used?

____

____

____

____

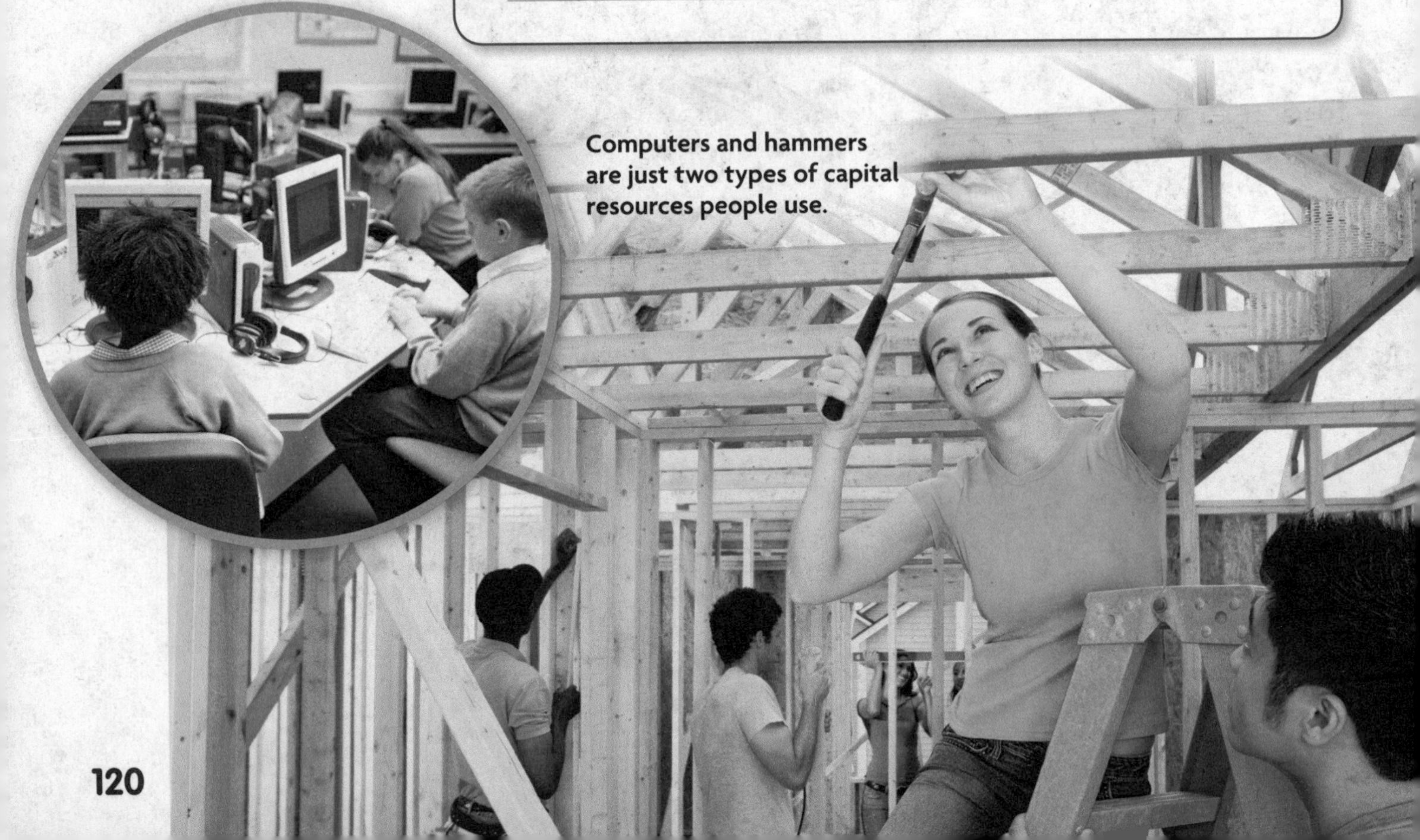

Computers and hammers are just two types of capital resources people use.

(l)Tim Platt/The Image Bank/Getty Images,(r)Photodisc/Getty Images

farm machinery

steel

server

factory workers

grains

wood

How Capital Resources are Used

Capital resources are used to create another good or service. Think about the types of capital resources in your city. There are many cars that people use to travel around town. By itself, a car is not a capital resource. If a car is used as a taxi, however, it is considered a capital resource. A person pays someone to drive them somewhere in the city. The car has been used to create a service.

The chart above shows some of the different natural, human, and capital resources in the United States. Are there any resources from your community that you could add to this chart?

How are capital resources used?

Technology

Changes in technology have also affected our lives as buyers and sellers. Producers now rely on robot-powered assembly lines to make cars. A grocery store needs UPC barcodes to appear on their products so it's easier and quicker to check out the buyers. Online shopping has also made shopping more convenient.

Write a plan for your own business. Explain what good or service you will provide and what resources you will need.

_____

_____

_____

_____

Lesson 2

? Essential Question Why are resources important?

_____

_____

_____

_____

Go back to *Show As You Go!* on pages 102–103.

networks
connected.mcgraw-hill.com
● Games ● Assessment

Scarcity and Trade

 Essential Question

How does scarcity affect trade?

What do you think?

_____

_____

_____

_____

Words To Know

Write what you think each word means on the lines.

demand _____

_____

supply _____

_____

scarcity _____

_____

*product _____

_____

trade _____

_____

In the last lesson, you read about buyers and sellers. Aaron is a buyer. He wants to buy the new SuperQuest video game, but it has been sold out for weeks!

Reading Skill

Analyze Visuals

Use the picture to explain what is happening on these pages.

_____

_____

_____

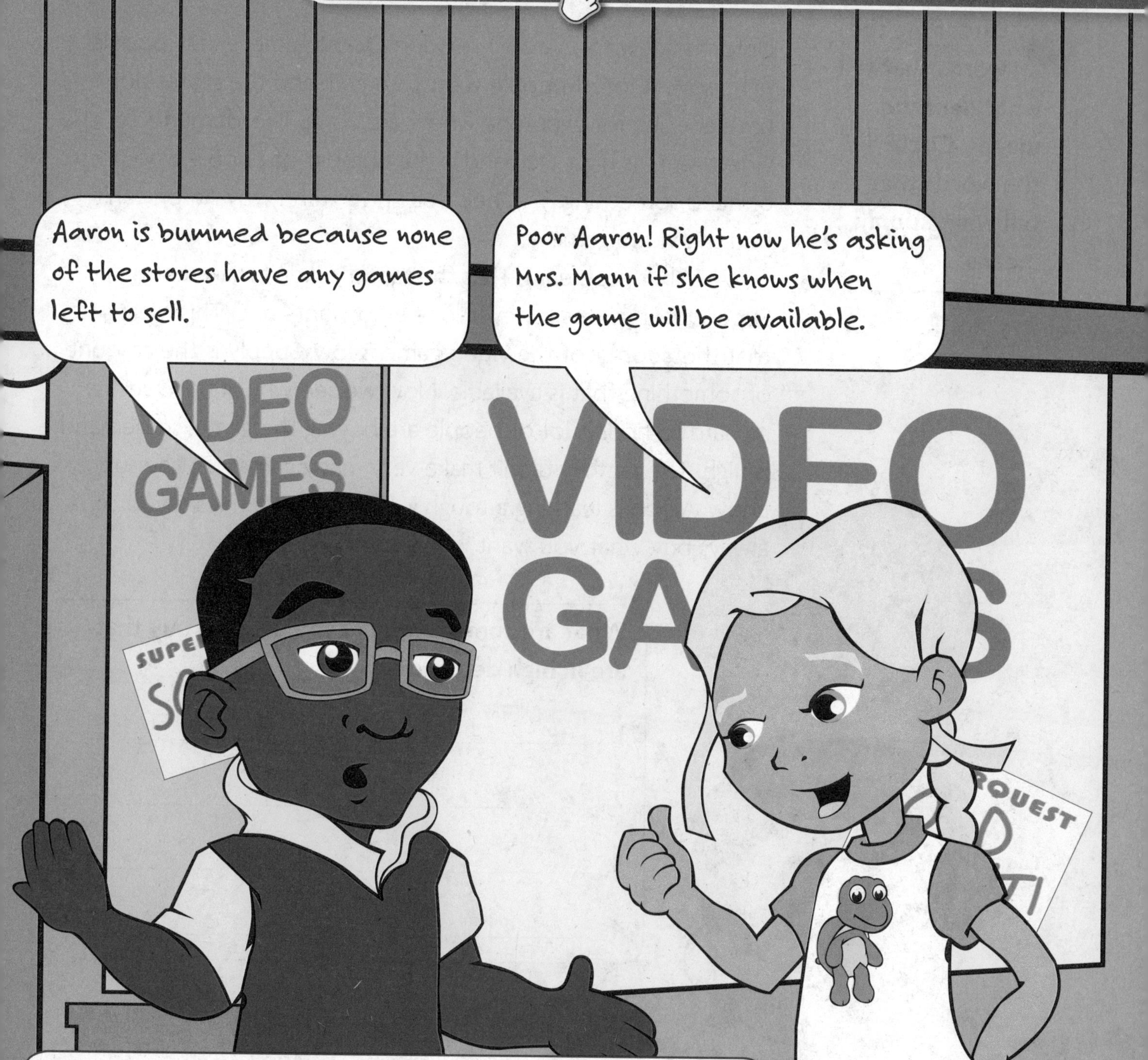

Aaron is bummed because none of the stores have any games left to sell.

Poor Aaron! Right now he's asking Mrs. Mann if she knows when the game will be available.

What would you do if you wanted to buy something and it was sold out?

_____

_____

_____

_____

Supply, Demand, and Scarcity

Underline the words that tell what *demand* means. (Circle) the words that tell what *supply* means.

Unfortunately for Aaron, the SuperQuest game is very popular right now. A lot of people want to buy it, and the stores don't have enough for everyone who wants one. The **demand** for the video game is high. Demand is the number of people who want or need something. This helps us understand why Aaron can't find the video game.

Another problem is that the factory didn't make enough SuperQuest games for everyone who wants one. This means that the **supply** of the video game is low. Supply is the amount of something that is available. Now we see why SuperQuest is so hard to find! A lot of people are buying the game, so demand is high. The factory didn't make very many games, so the supply is low. Aaron is learning a tough lesson in economics—you can't always buy what you want when you want it.

What are some products you want to buy that are in high demand?

1. _____

2. _____

3. _____

4. _____

When there is a low supply of an item, we say the item is scarce. **Scarcity** is when an item is difficult to find or get. When a **product** that you want to buy is scarce, you have to make choices. The people selling the scarce product might charge a high price for it. Do you pay the high price? Or do you wait until the price goes down? Maybe you decide not to buy the product at all!

Another choice might be to **trade** for the item you want. To trade means to give one item in return for something else. When things are scarce, people may trade with each other for items they want or need.

Reading Skill

Cause and Effect Underline what happens when a product is scarce.

Imagine that you have a SuperQuest game that you will trade with Aaron. Draw what you would accept from him in return.

Products Traded in the United States

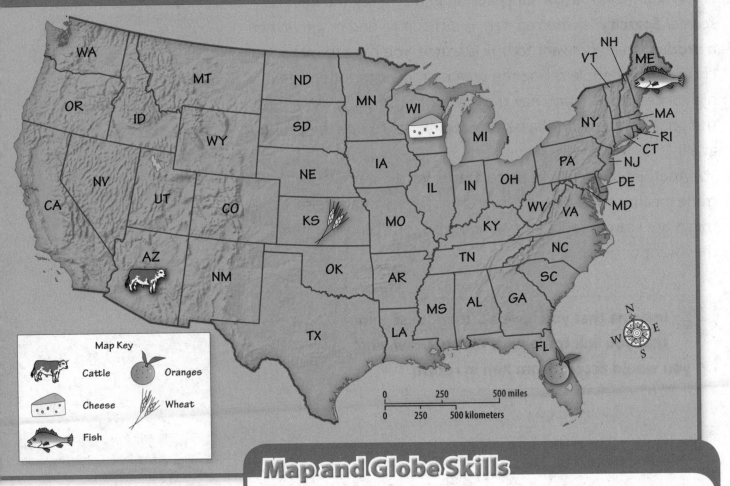

Map Key
- Cattle
- Cheese
- Fish
- Oranges
- Wheat

WA, OR, ID, MT, ND, MN, WI, MI, NY, VT, NH, ME, MA, RI, CT, NJ, DE, MD, PA, OH, IN, IL, IA, SD, WY, NV, CA, UT, CO, NE, KS, MO, KY, WV, VA, NC, OK, AR, TN, SC, AZ, NM, TX, LA, MS, AL, GA, FL

0 250 500 miles
0 250 500 kilometers

Map and Globe Skills

What information can you learn from this map?

Trade in the United States

Trade isn't just for toys and video games. States trade for products, too! The Southeast is known for growing citrus fruits, such as oranges. Because oranges grow well, people can easily find them in stores and markets.

But other products are not as easy to find in the Southeast. They are scarce. How do we get these scarce items? We trade for them! We sell the products we have, and we buy the products we need. So while we eat products such as cheese, wheat, or beef from other states, people in those states eat oranges grown in the Southeast.

Resources and Trade

We trade for scarce resources, too. One example of a scarce resource is oil. It is only found in certain areas of the world, and there is a limited supply. We use oil for many different things, including gas for our cars and trucks. We have to trade with other states—or even other countries—to get this scarce resource.

Suppose you are reading a about scarcity on farms in the United States. You come to a diagram like the one below. It is a **line graph**. A line graph shows information that changes over time. Let's see how to get information from a line graph.

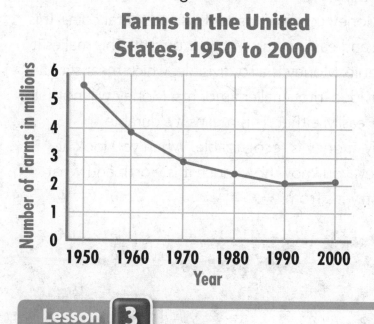

Farms in the United States, 1950 to 2000

Lesson 3

? **Essential Question** How does scarcity affect trade?

_____

_____

_____

_____

_____

Go back to *Show As You Go!* on pages 102–103.

Currency in North America and the Caribbean

? Essential Question

Why is money important?
What do you think?

_____

_____

_____

_____

_____

_____

_____

_____

Words To Know

Ⓒircle the words you know. Put a **?** next to the words you don't know.

characteristic

*feature

currency

symbol

You've learned that most people use money when they buy or sell products. Money has many **characteristics** that make it easy to use. A characteristic is a **feature** that helps us identify something.

Money comes in paper bills and metal coins. It is small and easy to carry in your pocket. This makes it portable. Money is also divisible, which means it can be divided into smaller amounts. Money will not fall apart easily, either. This means it's durable. Finally, money is recognizable. When you look at money, you know how much it is worth and what country it's from.

Underline the characteristics of money.

Every country in the world has a money system called **currency**. Currency is different from one country to the next. The names of the bills and coins are different. For example, in the United States, we call paper money "dollars." In Mexico, paper money is called "pesos."

Currency also comes in different amounts, depending on which country it is from. You can trade one country's currency for another country's currency, too. This way, people all over the world can buy, sell, and trade with one another.

Make a list of ways to use money.

1. _____

2. _____

3. _____

4. _____

FUN FACTS
- A U.S. dollar bill can be folded more than 4,000 times before it will tear.
- A coin can last around 30 years.
- A million dollars in pennies would weigh nearly 500,000 pounds!

Currency Used in North America

The different currencies used in North America and the Caribbean all have some characteristics in common. They all have **symbols** on them. A symbol is a picture that represents something else. They also have words or numbers that tell you how much the currency is worth. But each currency has features that make it recognizable to each country. Let's take a look!

The United States

Paper currency in the United States is called "dollars." These paper bills are all the same size, but they are worth different amounts. The $1 bill, which has a picture of our first President on it, shows the number "1." This means that it is worth one dollar.

U.S. coins come in different values, too. Unlike paper bills, coins come in different shapes and sizes. Coins show a person on the front and a building, animal, or other symbol on the back. The value is written on the coin, too.

Canada

The paper currency in Canada is also called "dollars." Canadian paper bills are the same shape and size, but they are different colors. The fronts of the bills show important people in Canada's history. The backs show different symbols of Canada.

Canadian coins come in different colors and sizes, too. The coins have a picture of a person on the front. On the back are pictures of different plants or animals found in Canada. The value of each coin is also written on the back.

Mexico

Paper currency in Mexico is called "pesos." Pesos are the same size and shape, but they come in different colors. They have pictures of people and places that symbolize Mexico's history. Presidents, leaders, and even artists are featured on pesos. A number on the bill shows its value.

Most Mexican coins are called *centavos.* They come in different shapes and colors. They have a golden eagle on one side. The golden eagle is the national symbol of Mexico. There are also coins for 1, 2, 5, and 10 pesos. All of the peso coins have rings of steel around them.

The Caribbean

The Caribbean has many kinds of currency. Some Caribbean islands were settled by European countries. These islands use the same currency as those European countries. Other island countries are controlled by Britain. These countries joined currencies to create the East Caribbean dollar.

How can you recognize East Caribbean currency? East Caribbean coins show a picture of the British queen on one side. The front of all East Caribbean paper bills also show a picture of the queen. The other side shows the value, when the currency was made, and the words "East Caribbean States." Some East Caribbean coins also have a picture of a boat on them.

Reading Skill

Compare and Contrast

Circle the characteristics that show how these four currencies are similar. Underline the characteristics that show how they are different.

Match the Money

How well do you know the currency used in North America and the Caribbean? Match each bill or coin by drawing a line from it to the country or region where it is used. Good luck!

Create Your Own Currency

Now it's your turn to create a currency! Imagine that you have been asked to create a coin which will be used only in your state. In the space below, use what you have learned about currency to design your coin. Be sure to include pictures or symbols that represent your state in your design.

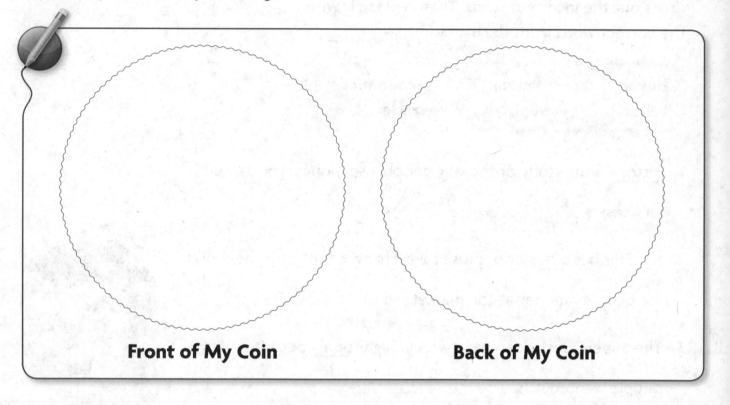

Front of My Coin   **Back of My Coin**

Lesson 3

? Essential Question   Why is money important?

_____

_____

_____

_____

Go back to *Show As You Go!* on pages 102–103. ◄◄◄

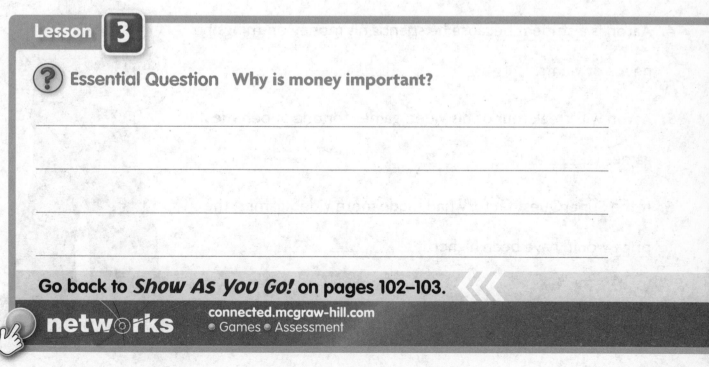

networks connected.mcgraw-hill.com
● Games ● Assessment

The underlined word in each sentence is incorrect.
Cross out the incorrect word. Then replace it with
the correct word from the list below.

buyer	demand	economics
seller	supply	trade

1. History is the study of the way people use money, goods, and

   services. _____

2. Mr. Smith is a farmer because he exchanges the goods he grows

   for people's money at the market. _____

3. The SuperQuest video game was in high supply because many

   people wanted it. _____

4. Aaron is a student because he spends his money on things he

   needs or wants. _____

5. Aaron will break four of his video games for one SuperQuest

   game. _____

6. If the SuperQuest factory had made more video games, the

   price would have been higher. _____

Unit Project

Think about what you have learned about economics in this unit. For your unit project, create your own advertisement. You can choose to sell anything you want. Use the previous pages to review what you've learned and apply it to your project. Read the list below to see what should be included in your advertisement.

Your advertisement should...   **Yes it does!**

show what good or service you are selling. ☐

encourage people to buy your product. ☐

explain what currency you will accept for your product. ☐

explain what you want in trade for your product. ☐

use at least two vocabulary terms from this unit. ☐

be colorful and fun! ☐

Think about the Big Idea

BIG IDEA Economics affects people.

What have you learned about how economics affects people?

_____

_____

_____

_____

Read the article "Trading with Other Countries" before answering Numbers 1 through 6.

Trading with Other Countries

by Adam Jones

Buyers and sellers in the United States work together to make goods and provide services. But we cannot make everything we need, so we have to trade with other countries. We trade the goods and services we have for the goods and services we need.

The United States sends its goods and resources to countries all over the world. It also brings in goods and resources from other countries. This system of trade helps the economies of all countries.

States also play an important part in the economy of the United States. For example, Florida trades goods including fruit, phosphates, and machine parts to countries around the world. In return, Florida receives wood from Canada, oil from Africa, and computers and other machines from Japan.

1 By reading the article and looking at the map, you can tell that Canada trades

Ⓐ oil.

Ⓑ clothing.

Ⓒ computers.

Ⓓ wood.

2 Which sentence from the article tells the main idea?

Ⓕ *Florida plays an important part in the economy of the United States.*

Ⓖ *We trade the goods and services we have for the goods and services we need.*

Ⓗ *The United States sends its goods and resources to countries all over the world.*

Ⓘ *Buyers and sellers in the United States work together to make goods and provide services.*

3 How is the system of trade in Florida SIMILAR to the system of trade in the United States?

Ⓐ They both trade goods with countries around the world.

Ⓑ They both trade services with Canada.

Ⓒ They both trade goods with buyers in Japan.

Ⓓ They both trade goods with sellers in Italy.

4 Which of the following is something that all countries of the world have in common?

Ⓕ oil

Ⓖ wool

Ⓗ gold

Ⓘ trade

5 What is the MOST LIKELY reason the author wrote this article?

Ⓐ to explain how Florida produces goods

Ⓑ to explain why the United States trades

Ⓒ to explain what goods Florida trades

Ⓓ to explain how goods are transported during trades

6 Which product does Florida ship to other countries?

Ⓕ oil

Ⓖ phosphates

Ⓗ computers

Ⓘ wool

UNIT 4 Government and Civics

BIG IDEA Rules provide order.

Think about the rules you must follow each day. Why do we need rules? How would things be different if we didn't have rules? The laws of our country can be a lot like the rules we follow at home or in school. In this unit, you will learn why government is needed and how it is organized. You will learn about the leaders of our country, of your state, and of your community. You will also learn that a leader's values and beliefs can affect our laws. How can your values and beliefs affect the laws in your community?

networks

There's More Online!

- Skill Builders
- Vocabulary Flashcards

Royalty-Free/CORBIS

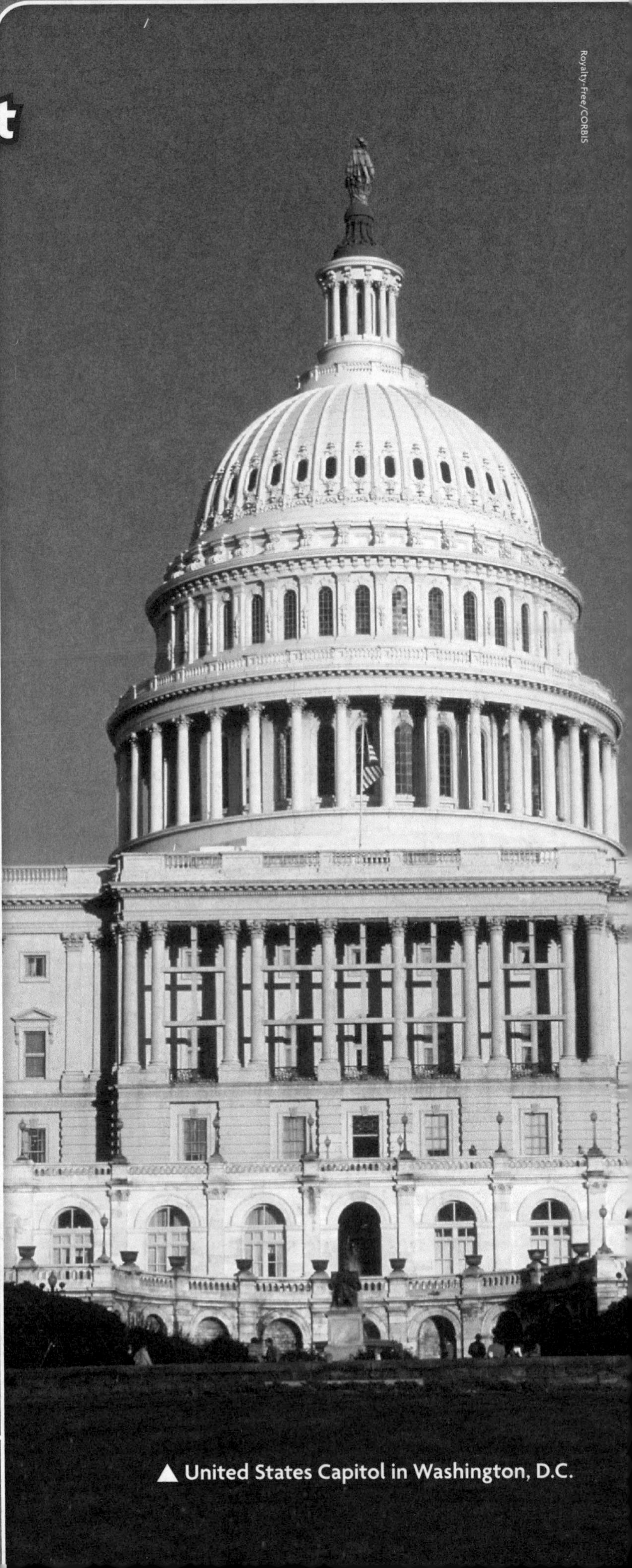

▲ United States Capitol in Washington, D.C.

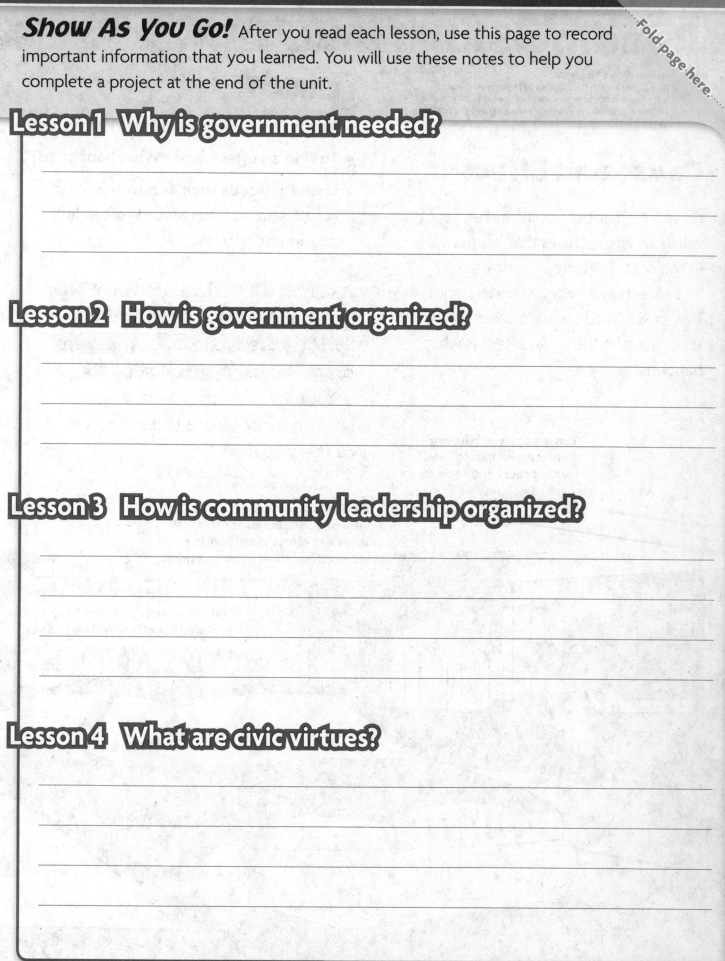

Show As You Go! After you read each lesson, use this page to record important information that you learned. You will use these notes to help you complete a project at the end of the unit.

Fold page here.

Lesson 1   Why is government needed?

_____

_____

_____

Lesson 2   How is government organized?

_____

_____

_____

Lesson 3   How is community leadership organized?

_____

_____

_____

_____

Lesson 4   What are civic virtues?

_____

_____

_____

_____

Reading Skill

Common Core Standards
RI.3 Describe the relationship between a series of historical events, scientific ideas or concepts, or steps in technical procedures in a text, using language that pertains to time, sequence, and cause/effect.

Cause and Effect

As you read about social studies, you will learn about things that happened in the past. Thinking about causes and effects will help you understand events you read about. A cause is why something happens. An effect is what happens.

LEARN IT

- To find a cause, ask, "Why did it happen?"
- To find an effect, ask, "What happened?"
- Look for words such as *because, as a result,* and *so.* These words often link causes and effects.

A citizen felt the intersection of Main Street and Palm Avenue was not safe. So, she talked to local government about putting a stop sign on the corner. People can safely cross the street now because traffic must stop at the stop sign.

This is a cause. It tells why something happened. Find another cause and circle it.

The words "as a result" and "so" are clue words. These words often link causes and effects. Find another clue word and draw a box around it.

This effect tells you what happened. Find another effect and underline it.

142

A graphic organizer can help you understand the relationship between causes and effects. Fill in the chart with causes and effects from the story on page 134.

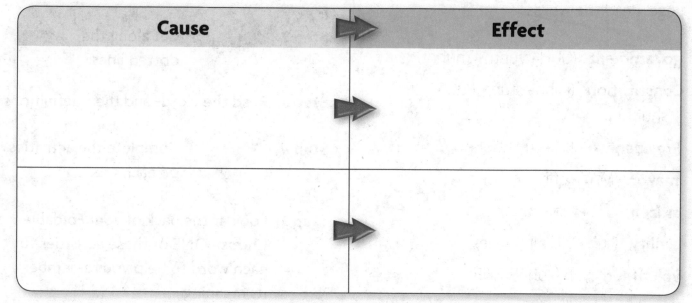

Cause		Effect

Leland Bobbe/Digital Vision/Getty Images

APPLY IT

- Review the steps for finding causes and effects in the Learn It section.

- Read the paragraph below. Then circle the causes and underline the effects in the passage.

A wind storm blew through Sanford on Friday. Mrs. Silva needed help to remove a tree in her yard because the tree was damaged during the storm. Mrs. Silva could not remove the tree alone. So, volunteers came to help her clean up and remove the tree on Saturday.

Words to Know

Common Core Standards
RI.4 Determine the meaning of general academic and domain-specific words and phrases in a text relevant to a grade 3 topic or subject area.

The list below shows some important words you will learn in this unit. Their definitions can be found on the next page. Read the words.

government (GUH • vuhrn • muhnt)

Constitution (kahn • stuh • TOO • shuhn)

President (PREH • zuh • duhnt)

mayor (MAY • uhr)

citizen (SIH • tuh • zuhn)

civility (suh • VIH • luh • tee)

volunteer (vah • luhn • TIHR)

cooperation (koh • ah • puh • RAY • shuhn)

The **Foldable** on the next page will help you learn these important words. Follow the steps below to make your Foldable.

Step 1 Fold along the solid red line.

Step 2 Cut along the dotted lines.

Step 3 Read the words and their definitions.

Step 4 Complete the activities on each tab.

Step 5 Look at the back of your Foldable. Choose ONE of these activities for each word to help you remember its meaning:

- Draw a picture of the word.
- Write a description of the word.
- Write how the word is related to something you know.

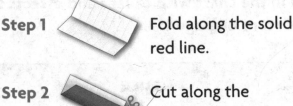

CONGRESS, JULY 4,

States of

We the People of the Uni

insure domestic Tranquility, provide for the common defence, promo
and our Posterity, do ordain and establish this Constitution for the U

(l)John Neubauer/PhotoEdit, (r)Jon Helgason/Alamy

| | | |

A **government** is all the people who run a community, state, or country.

Write a sentence using the word *government*.

The **President** is the leader of our country.

Circle the words that belong with the word *President*.

map   nation   street

metal   cause   leader

The **Constitution** is the plan for our nation's government.

Write a sentence using the word *Constitution*.

A **mayor** is the leader of a local government.

Write a sentence using the word *mayor*.

A **citizen** is a person who is a member of a community, state, or country.

Describe a citizen in your own words.

Civility is showing respect and kindness.

Write a synonym for the word *civility*.

A **volunteer** is a person who chooses to do a job without getting paid.

List two places in a community where people volunteer.

_____   _____

Cooperation is working together to meet goals.

Write about a time you used cooperation.

government	government
President	President
Constitution	Constitution
mayor	mayor
citizen	citizen
civility	civility
volunteer	volunteer
cooperation	cooperation

✂ CUT HERE

146

Primary Sources

Documents

Documents are important primary sources. They tell us about the laws and agreements people made in the past. You can use documents to understand more about our laws and our government. One way to study documents is to read them. You can also use video or audio recordings to listen to what was written in a document.

In this unit, you will learn about our government's documents. One of these documents is the Preamble—the beginning of the U.S. Constitution. It is important because it explains what our government is supposed to do. As you read, think about when and why the Preamble was written. Why do you think it is an important document?

Primary Source

We the people of the United States, in order to form a more perfect union, establish justice, insure domestic tranquility, provide for the common defense, promote the general welfare, and secure the blessings of liberty to ourselves and our posterity, do ordain and establish this Constitution for the United States of America.

—The Preamble of the U.S. Constitution

DBQ Document-Based Questions

Read the Preamble on the right. Then complete the activities below.

1. Circle the words that explain who wrote the Preamble to the Constitution.

2. How can reading documents help you learn more about our laws?

_____

_____

_____

networks
connected.mcgraw-hill.com
● Skill Builders
● Resource Library

Lesson 1 Government

? Essential Question

Why is government important?
What do you think?

_____

_____

_____

_____

_____

Words To Know

Draw a symbol on each line to show how much you know about the meaning of each word.

? = I have no idea!
▲ = I know a little.
★ = I know a lot!

____ **government**

____ **representative democracy**

____ ***establish**

Rules and Laws

Have you ever been in a classroom discussion where everyone was talking at once? Maybe you had something you wanted to say, but nobody was listening. Or maybe you couldn't hear because of all the noise. It's hard to pay attention when we all talk at once. It is a lot easier to discuss things when people take turns speaking. Classroom rules help us have better discussions. They also help us get along in other ways at school.

> **What is one rule that would change how students are acting in this picture?**
>
> _____

Ryan McVay/Digital Vision/Getty Images

148

Communities have rules, too. These rules are called laws. Laws come from our **government**. A government is all the people who run a community, state, or country. Governments make laws to keep communities safe, healthy, and organized. What rules do you follow to stay organized at school?

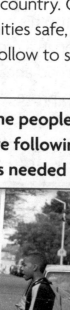

The people pictured on this page are following laws. Write why each law is needed below each picture.

Draw a picture of you following a law.

Safety and Services

You know that cars must stop at red lights and may only drive ahead on green lights. That's a law the government created. What would happen if drivers did not obey this important law? People might have accidents and get hurt.

Traffic signs show laws, too. A driver must stop his or her car at a red stop sign. A yellow sign with a person in a crosswalk shows drivers that people may be crossing the road ahead. Our government creates these signs and laws to help protect people. These laws promote safety and organization.

TRAFFIC LIGHT FACTS!

Driving through a red light can cost a driver over $300!

How long a yellow light stays lit depends on the speed limit.

Green doesn't mean "go"— it means "cross with caution."

Shawn McKelvey

THINK • PAIR • SHARE
Think about how your street sign would keep people safe and organized. Share your ideas with a partner.

Like traffic lights, street signs help us stay safe. Design your own street sign below.

Our government doesn't just promote safety and organization by creating laws. It also provides many different services. Police officers keep streets, highways, and neighborhoods safe. Firefighters protect us and our property from fire damage. City workers clean our streets and collect garbage, which helps to keep us healthy. Just imagine what our lives would be like if trash piled up in the street!

Some government services help people do work or improve their lives. The United States Postal Service delivers our mail all over the world. Public libraries across our country provide access to information. They are paid for by our government. Public schools are provided by the government, too, to make sure everyone gets an education!

Write the service that is being provided on the line below each picture.

Reading Skill

Meaning of Words

Promote is a word that means to support or put forward. What is one rule you could promote in your school?

_____

_____

_____

People Power

It might seem like our government makes all the laws, and the people don't have any say. But that isn't true! In our country, the government gains its power from the people. How does this work?

When the Founders of the United States were creating a new government, they decided the government should be run by the people. The government they created is a **representative democracy**. In a representative democracy, the people vote for a group of leaders. These leaders represent the people. They **establish** the rules and laws for everyone to follow.

How do the people choose their leaders? Write it on the arrow!

Get Out and Vote

Now we know that government leaders are elected by the people. But how do they keep their jobs as leaders? If people think their leaders are doing a good job, they vote for them again. If people think their leaders are doing a bad job, they vote for someone else. One day, you will be able to vote. The people you vote for will make laws that affect you!

What would our government be like if the people didn't elect their leaders?

_____

_____

_____

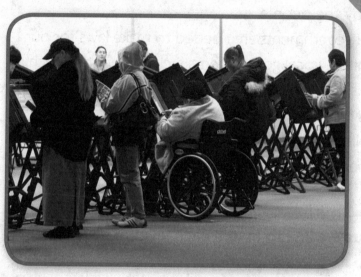

▲ Today almost every legal resident of the United States who is 18 or older can vote.

(l) McGraw-Hill Education, (r) Ed-Imaging

Lesson 1

(?) **Essential Question** Why is government important?

_____

_____

_____

_____

Go back to _Show As You Go!_ on pages 132–133. ◀◀

Three Levels of Government

How are people governed?
What do you think?

_____

_____

_____

_____

Words To Know

(Circle) the words you know.
Put a **?** next to the words
you don't know.

Constitution

*entire

President

supreme

governor

mayor

Working for the People

In the United States, there are three levels of government.
We have local government, state government, and federal
government, which is government for the whole country.
Each level of government has its own leaders who are
elected by the people.

   Local governments are needed to make laws for our
communities. Local governments include counties, such as
Hendricks, or cities, such as Danville. Like Indiana, every state
has its own state government. Indiana's state government
is found in their state capital—Indianapolis. The federal
government is in our nation's capital—Washington, D.C.

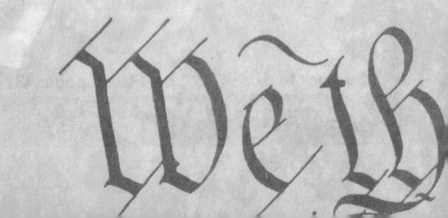

**Draw a line to match each level of government
to its correct location.**

Federal Government •   • **Danville**

Local Government •   • **Indiana**

State Government •   • **Washington, D.C.**

A Plan for Government

Our country's first leaders wanted to establish a plan for our national government that would keep people safe and free. So, they wrote the United States **Constitution**. This document contains the most important laws that everyone in our country must follow. It also explains how the government is organized. The Constitution says that our **entire** country is to be led by a leader called the **President**. The laws in the Constitution also protect our basic freedoms, or rights. Here are some of our rights found in the Constitution:

> **DID YOU KNOW?**
> The U.S. Constitution was written in 1787. It is the oldest Constitution still in use by any country in the world.

- *The right to practice any religion.*
- *The right to meet peacefully in groups.*
- *The right to say what we think.*
- *The right to write what we think.*
- *The right to be treated fairly under the law.*

Local and state governments must protect these rights. This is because the U.S. Constitution is the **supreme** law of the land. The word *supreme* means the most important. This means the U.S. Constitution includes laws that everyone in the United States must follow.

Reading Skill

Ask and Answer Questions How was the government of the United States established?

_____

_____

_____

_____

Jon Helgason/Alamy

State Government

Each state has its own constitution, too. State constitutions are a lot like the U.S. Constitution. All state constitutions have to follow the laws in the U.S. Constitution. However, each state has its own needs that might be different from the needs of the country. Because of this, each state constitution has rules and laws that are special for that state.

State constitutions say that every state should have a **governor**. The governor is the leader of a state and has many different jobs to do. The governor makes sure that the state laws are followed and decides how to spend state money. The governor decides how much money to spend on programs that help make a better place to live, work, and play.

(l)Alex Wong/Hulton Archive/Getty Images, (r)Carol M. Highsmith/Library of Congress Prints and Photographs Division

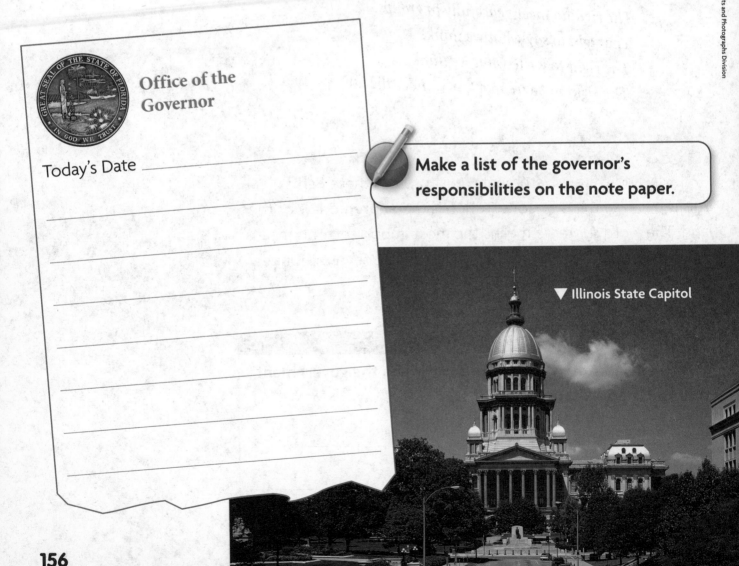

Office of the Governor

Today's Date _____

_____

_____

_____

_____

_____

_____

_____

Make a list of the governor's responsibilities on the note paper.

▼ Illinois State Capitol

People in communities pay taxes. A tax is money paid to the government. State governments collect taxes, too. This money pays for services provided by a state's government. These include keeping highways safe and clean. States also run health programs and state colleges. We are lucky because the state also gives cities and towns money to help buy books and software for their local schools!

State governments also work to protect the environment. States set aside land to preserve natural resources or to protect plants and animals. This means houses or other buildings cannot be built on the land. State parks, such as the Roaring River State Park, are places where visitors can see wildlife and enjoy the outdoors. State parks are run and paid for by state governments.

Match the numbers on each picture with the correct state service.

Highway Maintenance _____

State Parks _____

Public Education _____

Local Government

Who hires fire fighters and police officers? And who makes sure that the trash is picked up and checks that the traffic lights work? Your local government does all these things! Local governments are made up of the people who run a county, city, or town. Local government is the level of government that most closely affects our everyday lives.

The leader of a city or town is usually called a **mayor**. Mayors make sure that local laws are followed. They work to solve problems that affect their community. They also decide how a community's tax money is spent. People who live and work in a community pay taxes to local governments. Local governments then use the tax money to pay for the services the community needs. They hire people to pave roads, collect trash and recyclables, and run libraries and parks.

Stockbyte/Getty Images

Reading Skill
Cause and Effect **Underline the effect of paying taxes to local government.**

Local Government in Action

The mayor and other city leaders decide how money should be spent. This diagram shows some of the services local governments provide.

Use these words to label the diagram.

traffic safety
parks
fire protection
libraries
road repair
local museums

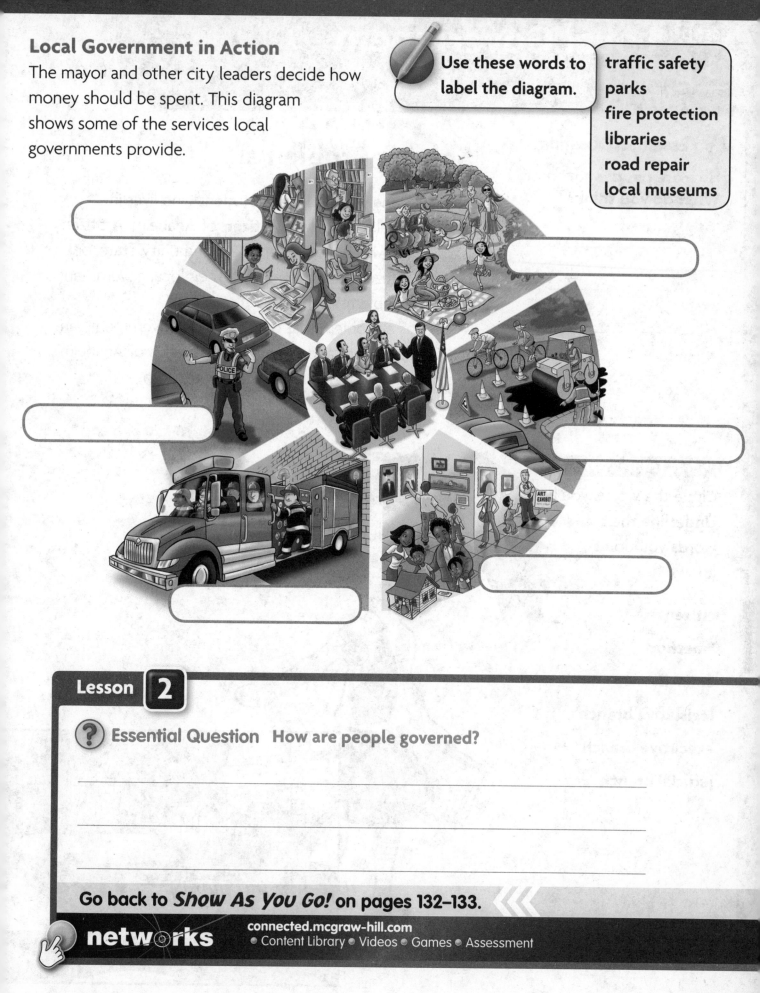

Lesson 2

? Essential Question How are people governed?

_____

_____

_____

Go back to _Show As You Go!_ on pages 132–133. «

networks   connected.mcgraw-hill.com
● Content Library ● Videos ● Games ● Assessment

159

Local Government

Words To Know

(Circle) the words you know.
Underline the words you don't know.

citizen

*method

council

legislative branch

executive branch

judicial branch

Solving Problems

This is Jill. She is a third-grade student who lives in Anaheim, California. Jill is a **citizen** of Anaheim. A citizen is a person who is a member of a community, state, or country. Citizens often work with their local government to solve problems in their city.

Jill has a problem that only the local government can fix. Read her story and see how each branch of Anaheim's local government helps her with her concern.

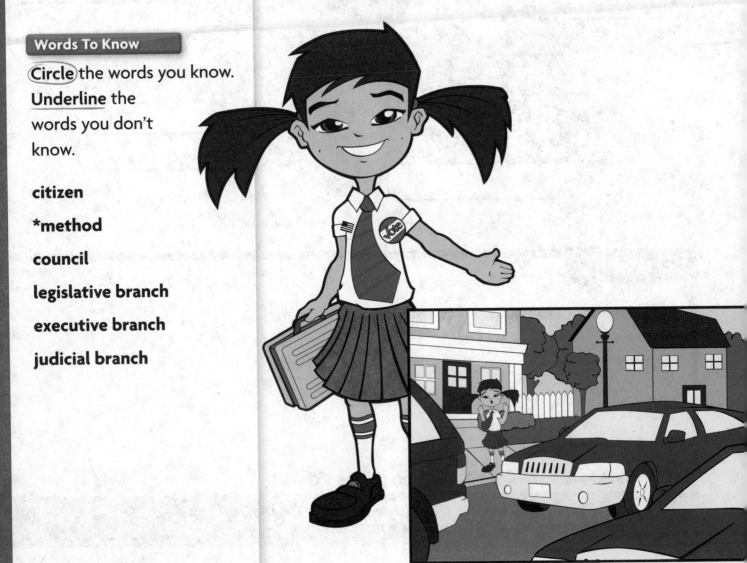

©Purestock/Alamy

◀ Traffic laws help keep
this intersection safe.

Like the intersection above, the corner where Jill's school bus stops is very busy. Jill thinks her bus stop is not safe. Cars drive by without stopping. Crossing the street near her bus stop is very dangerous.

Jill talks about the problem with her father. Jill and her father think a stop sign will make the corner safer. It is a law that cars must stop at a stop sign. But Jill and her father cannot put a stop sign up on their own. One **method** for improving community safety is to talk to local government.

Draw a picture to show what happens next.

161

What the People Want

First, Jill and her father talk to their neighbors. They explain the problem. They ask their neighbors to sign a petition to give to the local government. A petition is a special letter that many people sign. The petition says that people want a stop sign at the corner near Jill's bus stop.

Write the beginning of Jill's petition.

_____

_____

_____

_____

Next, Jill and her father go to a city **council** meeting in Anaheim. A council is a group of people who make the laws for a community. The city council is the **legislative branch** of local government. The legislative branch makes the laws. Some cities have a city commission instead of a council, but they do the same kind of work.

The city council often meets to talk about city problems. The council makes laws to help solve these problems. The people of the city must follow the laws.

Citizens may speak about problems at council meetings. Jill is going to speak at today's council meeting. She wants to explain the problem in her neighborhood and ask the council for a stop sign.

▲ a city council

Reading Skill

Point of View

A point of view is what the author is trying to explain or describe. Sometimes our opinion can be different from that of another person. Write the point of view of someone who does not agree with Jill.

_____

_____

_____

_____

Getting Things Done

The city council listens to Jill's speech. They read the petition other citizens have signed. Then they talk about the problem. The city council decides to hold a vote on the new stop sign. Every member of the council votes to approve Jill's plan!

The mayor is at the city council meeting. As you learned in Lesson 2, mayors carry out local laws. Mayors are in the **executive branch** of local government. The executive branch makes sure laws are followed. After Jill's plan is approved, the mayor makes sure the new stop sign is placed.

Write what the mayor will tell city workers.

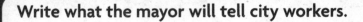

Today, cars must stop at the stop sign by Jill's bus stop. People who don't stop are breaking a law. They must pay a fine or go to court. Courts are part of a local government's **judicial branch**. The judicial branch decides if a law has been carried out fairly.

Courts are run by judges. Each county has a county court. If a police officer stops a car for driving by Jill's stop sign without stopping, the court will decide if the driver was breaking the law. State courts are called circuit courts.

Thanks to Jill, it is now safer to cross the street by her bus stop. Jill is glad that her local government helped her solve a problem in her community. What problems can you help solve in your community?

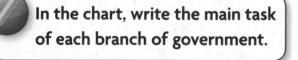

In the chart, write the main task of each branch of government.

Branches of Government

	Legislative
	Executive
	Judicial

BEVERLY O'NEILL, MAYO

Lesson 3

? **Essential Question** How are people governed?

_____

_____

_____

Go back to *Show As You Go!* on pages 132–133.

networks
connected.mcgraw-hill.com
• Games • Assessment

Good Citizens

Essential Question

How do people affect communities?

What do you think?

_____

_____

_____

_____

_____

Words To Know

Draw the symbol next to each word to show how much you know about the meaning of the word.

? = I have no idea!

▲ = I know a little.

★ = I know a lot.

____ **civility**

____ ***conduct**

____ **volunteer**

____ **cooperation**

____ **civic virtue**

Being a Good Citizen

In the last lesson, you read about how Jill is a good citizen. She helped get a new law passed in her community. The new law will keep people safe. People in her community must obey the new law. Obeying laws is one way to be a good citizen.

Good citizens can help people in many other ways. We can help others at home, at school, or in our communities. You will learn more about helping others in this lesson.

1. **Think about the picture below. Fill in the speech bubble with what a good citizen might say.**

2. **Civility** **means showing respect and kindness. How does your conduct show civility?**

_____

_____

Garth Glazier

Responsibility

When citizens follow rules and laws, they are showing responsibility. You are responsible when you follow rules at home or in school. Some rules and laws are made to keep us and others safe. It is everyone's responsibility to follow laws in their communities.

Andrew listens carefully when his teacher asks a question. He raises his hand when he knows the answer. Andrew is showing responsibility by following classroom rules.

Jenna walks her dog in the dog park. She keeps her dog on a leash. Jenna is showing responsibility by following park rules.

NO SKATEBOARDING ON SIDEWALK

Look at this sign about skateboarding. Explain how this law keeps people in the community safe.

_____

_____

_____

These citizens are helping their community.

Leland Bobbe/Digital Vision/Getty Images

Making a Difference

Underline who will make the laws that affect you.

You can make a difference at home, at school, or in your community. As you learned, showing responsibility is one way to be a good citizen. Voting for our leaders is a way to be a good citizen, too! Voting is a way for people to be involved and to make a difference. If you are a citizen, you will be able to vote one day. Remember, the people you vote for will make the laws that affect you.

Another way people can be involved and make a difference is to **volunteer**. A volunteer is a person who chooses to do a job without getting paid. People can volunteer to do many different things. Volunteers clean up neighborhoods and parks. Some volunteers collect canned food for local food banks. A food bank is a place that helps people who don't have enough to eat.

Make a list of ways you can volunteer.

1. _____

2. _____

3. _____

Maya wanted to volunteer to make a difference in her community. Read below to find out how Maya organized a book drive to collect books for a local hospital.

First, I asked the principal if I could organize a book drive at school. Together we decided our slogan for the book drive would be "A Good Book Is Good Medicine."

Next, my friends and I made posters and decorated boxes. We wanted people to know we were collecting books for Children's Hospital.

Finally, I sorted the books and took them to Children's Hospital. I made a big sign to say thank you to everyone who donated books to my book drive.

Draw a picture that shows Maya giving books to children at the hospital. Write how Maya feels about being a volunteer.

Working Together

Fill in the word web with examples of how people cooperate.

Think about Maya's book drive. Maya and her principal shared their ideas to create a slogan for the book drive. To make posters and decorate boxes, Maya and her friends had to share glue and markers. Sharing ideas and supplies are examples of **cooperation**. Cooperation means working together to meet goals.

Sometimes you might have a friend that doesn't want to cooperate. What would happen if Maya and her friends didn't share the glue and markers? That would cause a **conflict**, or a problem between two or more people. Teachers and parents can always help to solve a conflict. Sometimes a compromise, or agreement, can be made to solve the conflict. Someone may think they have a right to keep the glue and markers throughout the entire project. They have a different opinion than you. A teacher can help you to reach a compromise.

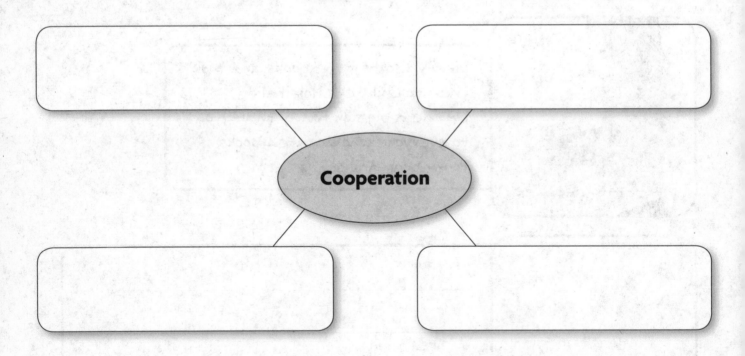

In this lesson, you learned about **civic virtues**. Civic virtues are people's actions that show civility, responsibility, and cooperation. As you have learned, being a volunteer is a civic virtue, too.

There are groups that work with volunteers. Habitat for Humanity is a volunteer organization that builds houses. Families who do not have the money to build their own house help the volunteers. The family and the volunteers cooperate to build the new house together.

John Neubauer / PhotoEdit

What civic virtues do you have?

_____

_____

_____

_____

Volunteers work together for Habitat for Humanity. ▼

Lesson **4**

(?) Essential Question How do people affect communities?

_____

_____

_____

_____

Go back to _Show As You Go!_ on pages 132–133. ⪡

networks
connected.mcgraw-hill.com
● Games ● Assessment

Write a letter on each line to match the words and phrases with their descriptions. Then write each word or phrase in the correct box it belongs in below.

____ 1. legislative branch

____ 2. civility

____ 3. state constitution

____ 4. government services

____ 5. representative democracy

____ 6. local government

____ 7. cooperation

____ 8. volunteer

A. a form of government where people vote for their leaders

B. the group of government leaders who make laws

C. working together to meet goals

D. someone who does a job without being paid

E. to show respect and kindness

F. the people who run a county, city, or town

G. police officers, firefighters, public libraries, and public schools

H. document which contains the rules and laws for states

Government	Good Citizens

Unit Project

Imagine that you have been elected to the class government. Your job is to write a new constitution for your class. What rules will you include? Who are the leaders, and what are their roles? Use the information you learned in this unit to help you write your constitution. Before you begin writing, look back at the previous pages to review your notes. As you work, check off each task.

Corbis

Your constitution should...   **Yes, it does!**

explain why rules are needed.   ☐

identify the leaders in your school.   ☐

describe the roles of those leaders.   ☐

explain the rights of administrators, teachers, and students. ☐

explain how those rights are protected.   ☐

promote civility, volunteerism, and cooperation.   ☐

Think about the Big Idea

BIG IDEA 💡 **Rules provide order.**

What have you learned about how rules provide order?

_____

_____

_____

_____

173

Read the article "Checks and Balances" before answering Numbers 1 through 8.

Checks and Balances

by Marcus Hatch

The government of the United States is divided into three branches. Each branch has its own job to do. The legislative branch (Congress) is in charge of making laws. The executive branch (the President) is in charge of carrying out the laws. The judicial branch (Supreme Court) makes sure the laws follow the Constitution. But each branch also has some power over the other branches. This system, called "checks and balances," was set up by the Founders to ensure that all parts of the government work together for the good of the American people.

How does this system work? Each branch is checked by the other two in different ways. For example, the President can say "no" to a bill passed by Congress. This is called a veto. But, Congress can override that veto if they have enough votes. In addition, the Supreme Court may check Congress by stating that a law is unconstitutional. The power is balanced because members of the Supreme Court are selected by the President. In addition, Congress has to approve the President's choices for the Supreme Court.

1 What is one responsibility of the legislative branch?

Ⓐ to make sure the laws follow the Constitution

Ⓑ to carry out the laws

Ⓒ to make laws for the country

Ⓓ to lead the military

2 Read this sentence from the article.

"In addition, the Supreme Court may check Congress by stating that a law is unconstitutional."

What is the meaning of the word *unconstitutional*?

Ⓕ illegal

Ⓖ broken

Ⓗ allowed

Ⓘ extreme

3 What is the purpose of this article?

ⓐ to explain the role of the Founders

ⓑ to explain how checks and balances work

ⓒ to explain the role of the legislative branch

ⓓ to explain how the United States' government is set up

4 Who is the leader of the executive branch?

ⓕ a member of Congress

ⓖ the President of the United States

ⓗ the Founders of our country

ⓘ the Supreme Court

5 What is the system that ensures government works together called?

ⓐ veto

ⓑ unconstitutional

ⓒ carrying out laws

ⓓ checks and balances

6 How does the legislative branch check the executive branch?

ⓕ It can say "no" to a bill passed by the judicial branch.

ⓖ It can state that a law is unconstitutional.

ⓗ It can select someone to serve on the Supreme Court.

ⓘ It can override a veto.

7 Why does the U.S. government have a system of checks and balances?

ⓐ to prevent the government from spending too much money

ⓑ to make sure each branch works together

ⓒ to keep the executive branch from carrying out laws

ⓓ to make sure the judicial branch has the most power

8 How are the executive and judicial branches ALIKE?

ⓕ They have checks over Congress.

ⓖ They can veto a law passed by Congress.

ⓗ Their members are chosen by Congress.

ⓘ They are more powerful than Congress.

Reference Section

Jessica Byrne

Geography and You

Geography is the study of Earth and the people, plants, and animals that live on it. Most people think of geography as learning about cities, states, and countries, but geography is far more. Geography includes learning about land, such as mountains and plains, and bodies of water, such as oceans, lakes, and rivers.

Geography includes the study of how people adapt to living in a new place. Geography is also about how people move around, how they move goods, and how ideas travel from place to place.

Dictionary of Geographic Terms

1 BAY Body of water partly surrounded by land

2 BEACH Land covered with sand or pebbles next to an ocean or lake

3 CANAL Waterway dug across the land to connect two bodies of water

4 CANYON Deep river valley with steep sides

5 CLIFF High steep face of rock

6 COAST Land next to an ocean

7 DESERT A dry environment with few plants and animals

8 GULF Body of water partly surrounded by land; larger than a bay

9 HARBOR Protected place by an ocean or river where ships can safely stay

10 HILL Rounded, raised landform; not as high as a mountain

11 ISLAND Land that is surrounded on all sides by water

12 **LAKE** Body of water completely surrounded by land	**17** **PLAIN** Large area of flat land
13 **MESA** Landform that looks like a high, flat table	**18** **PLATEAU** High flat area that rises steeply above the surrounding land
14 **MOUNTAIN** High landform with steep sides; higher than a hill	**19** **PORT** Place where ships load and unload goods
15 **OCEAN** Large body of salt water	**20** **RIVER** Long stream of water that empties into another body of water
16 **PENINSULA** Land that has water on all sides but one	**21** **VALLEY** Area of low land between hills or mountains

United States: Political

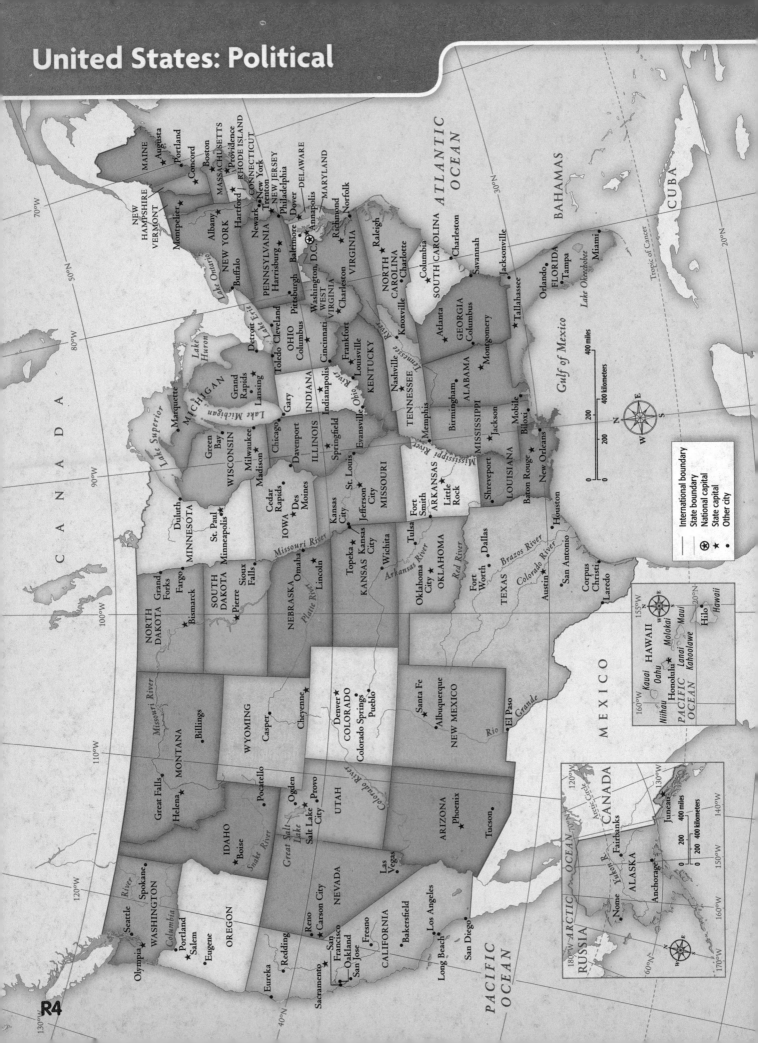

United States: Physical

Legend:
- Interational boundary
- State boundary
- ⊛ National capital
- ▲ Mountain peak
- ▲ Highest point
- ▶ Lowest point

ATLANTIC OCEAN

BAHAMA

CUBA

Florida Keys

Straits of Florida

ME

Mt. Washington 6,288 ft. (1,917 m) ▲

NH

VT

GREEN MOUNTAINS

MA

CT RI

Cape Cod

Long Island

NY

ADIRONDACK MOUNTAINS

St. Lawrence R.

Hudson

Lake Ontario

ALLEGHENY PLATEAU

PA

NJ

DE

MD

Delaware Bay

Washington, D.C. ⊛

Chesapeake Bay

Cape Hatteras

VA

WV

APPALACHIAN MOUNTAINS

PIEDMONT

ATLANTIC COASTAL PLAIN

NC

Mt. Mitchell 6,684 ft. (2,037 m) ▲

SC

GA

Savannah R.

FL

Lake Okeechobee

Chattahoochee R.

ALLEGHENY PLATEAU

OH

Ohio River

KY

TN

Tennessee River

AL

Alabama R.

MS

Mobile Bay

Gulf of Mexico

Mississippi River Delta

Tropic of Cancer

Lake Superior

Lake Huron

GREAT LAKES

Lake Michigan

MI

Lake Erie

WI

MN

MESABI RANGE

Lake of the Woods

Mississippi River

IL

Wabash River

IN

Missouri River

IA

CENTRAL PLAINS

MO

Ozark Plateau

OZARK PLATEAU

AR

OUACHITA MOUNTAINS

Arkansas River

INTERIOR PLAINS

Red River

LA

GULF COASTAL PLAIN

Galveston Bay

CANADA

C A N A D A

ND

SD

BLACK HILLS

NE

KS

OK

TX

Brazos River

Colorado River

EDWARDS PLATEAU

Red River

Pecos River

Rio Grande

MEXICO

M E X I C O

Gulf of California

Missouri River

GREAT PLAINS

G R E A T   P L A I N S

Platte River

MT

Granite Peak 12,799 ft. (3,901 m) ▲

WY

ID

ROCKY MOUNTAINS

R O C K Y   M O U N T A I N S

Mt. Elbert 14,433 ft. (4,399 m) ▲

Pikes Peak 14,110 ft. (4,301 m) ▲

CO

COLORADO PLATEAU

Kings Peak 13,528 ft. (4,123 m) ▲

WASATCH RANGE

UT

Great Salt Lake

GREAT SALT LAKE DESERT

Wheeler Peak 13,161 ft. (4,011 m) ▲

NM

CONTINENTAL DIVIDE

Humphreys Peak 12,633 ft. (3,851 m) ▲

AZ

Gila River

Colorado River

SONORAN DESERT

Guadalupe Peak 8,749 ft. (2,667 m) ▲

Salton Sea

MOJAVE DESERT

Death Valley 282 ft. (−86 m) ▶

Lake Mead

NV

GREAT BASIN

G R E A T   B A S I N

Lake Tahoe

Mt. Whitney 14,494 ft. (4,418 m) ▲

SIERRA NEVADA

CENTRAL VALLEY

CA

Channel Islands

San Francisco Bay

Cape Mendocino

COAST RANGES

C O A S T   R A N G E S

Mt. Shasta 14,162 ft. (4,317 m) ▲

CASCADE RANGE

Mt. Hood 11,239 ft. (3,426 m) ▲

OR

Snake River

COLUMBIA PLATEAU

Columbia R.

Mt. St. Helens 8,363 ft. (2,549 m) ▲

Mt. Rainier 14,410 ft. (4,392 m) ▲

WA

Puget Sound

PACIFIC OCEAN

Scale (main map):
- 400 miles
- 400 kilometers
- 200
- 200
- 0
- 0

Compass rose: N E S W

Hawaii inset:
HAWAII

Kauai

Niihau

Oahu

Molokai

Lanai

Maui

Kahoolawe

Hawaii

Mauna Kea 13,796 ft. (4,205 m) ▲

PACIFIC OCEAN

160°W

155°W

20°N

200 miles
100
200 kilometers
100
0
0

Alaska inset:
CANADA

Yukon River

BROOKS RANGE

ALASKA

Arctic Circle

ALASKA RANGE

Mt. McKinley 20,320 ft. (6,194 m) ▲

Gulf of Alaska

RUSSIA

Bering Sea

Bering Strait

Aleutian Islands

ARCTIC OCEAN

70°N

160°W

150°W

140°W

400 miles
200
400 kilometers
200
0
0

30°W

40°W

40°N

30°N

70°W

80°W

90°W

100°W

110°W

120°W

160°W

170°W

60°N

ASIA

EUROPE

140°E · 150°E · 160°E · 170°E · 180° · 170°W

60°N · 70°N · 80°N

20°E · 10°E · 0° · 10°W · 50°W · 20°W · 30°W

ARCTIC OCEAN

+ North Pole

Lincoln Sea

Greenland Sea

ICELAND

Chukchi Sea

Bering Strait

Bering Sea

Beaufort Sea

Baffin Bay

GREENLAND (Denmark)

Davis Strait

AK (U.S.)

Gulf of Alaska

YUKON

NORTHWEST TERRITORIES

NUNAVUT

Labrador Sea

NEWFOUNDLAND AND LABRADOR

Hudson Bay

CANADA

BRITISH COLUMBIA · ALBERTA · SASKATCHEWAN · MANITOBA

ONTARIO

QUÉBEC

PRINCE EDWARD ISLAND

NOVA SCOTIA

NEW BRUNSWICK

WA · MT · ND · MN

OR · ID · SD · WI · MI

Ottawa ⊛

ME

VT · NH

NY · MA · RI

CT

WY · IA

NV · UT · NE · IL · IN · OH · PA

NJ · DE · MD

ATLANTIC OCEAN

UNITED STATES

CO · KS · MO · WV · VA

Washington, D.C. ⊛

CA · AZ · NM · OK · AR · KY · TN · NC · SC

MS · AL · GA

TX · LA

BERMUDA (U.K.)

FL

PACIFIC OCEAN

Gulf of California

MEXICO

Gulf of Mexico

THE BAHAMAS

DOMINICAN REPUBLIC

PUERTO RICO (U.S.)

ST. KITTS AND NEVIS

ANTIGUA AND BARBUDA

CUBA

Mexico City ⊛

JAMAICA

HAITI

Caribbean Sea

DOMINICA

ST. LUCIA

ST. VINCENT & THE GRENADINES

BARBADOS

BELIZE

HONDURAS

GRENADA

TRINIDAD AND TOBAGO

GUATEMALA

NICARAGUA

EL SALVADOR

COSTA RICA

SOUTH AMERICA

PANAMA

0 · 250 · 500 miles

0 · 250 · 500 kilometers

N W E S

Equator

50°N · 40°N · 30°N · 20°N · 10°N · 0°

150°W · 140°W

130°W · 120°W · 110°W · 100°W · 90°W · 80°W · 70°W · 60°W

40°N · 30°N · 20°N · 10°N

40°W · 50°W

—— International boundary

— State boundary

⊛ National capital

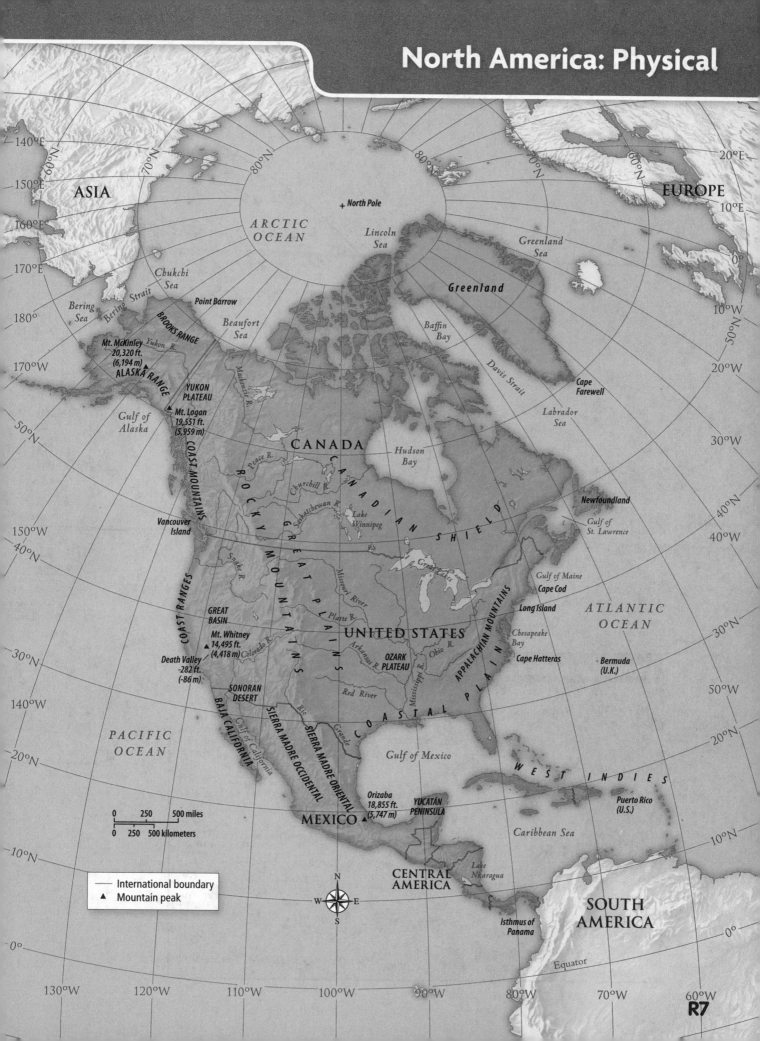

North America: Physical

ASIA

EUROPE

+ North Pole

ARCTIC OCEAN

Lincoln Sea

Greenland Sea

Chukchi Sea

Greenland

Bering Sea

Point Barrow

Baffin Bay

Beaufort Sea

BROOKS RANGE

Mt. McKinley 20,320 ft. (6,194 m)

ALASKA RANGE

Yukon R.

YUKON PLATEAU

Davis Strait

Cape Farewell

Gulf of Alaska

Mt. Logan 19,551 ft. (5,959 m)

COAST MOUNTAINS

Mackenzie R.

CANADA

Hudson Bay

Labrador Sea

Peace R.

ROCKY

CANADIAN SHIELD

Newfoundland

Churchill

Vancouver Island

Saskatchewan R.

MOUNTAINS

GREAT

Lake Winnipeg

Gulf of St. Lawrence

Snake R.

COAST RANGES

GREAT BASIN

Mt. Whitney 14,495 ft. (4,418 m)

Missouri River

Platte R.

PLAINS

Great Lakes

Gulf of Maine

Cape Cod

Long Island

ATLANTIC OCEAN

Death Valley -282 ft. (-86 m)

Colorado R.

UNITED STATES

Arkansas R.

OZARK PLATEAU

Ohio R.

APPALACHIAN MOUNTAINS

Chesapeake Bay

Cape Hatteras

Bermuda (U.K.)

SONORAN DESERT

BAJA CALIFORNIA

Gulf of California

SIERRA MADRE OCCIDENTAL

SIERRA MADRE ORIENTAL

Rio Grande

Red River

Mississippi R.

COASTAL

PLAIN

PACIFIC OCEAN

Gulf of Mexico

W E S T   I N D I E S

Puerto Rico (U.S.)

Orizaba 18,855 ft. (5,747 m)

YUCATÁN PENINSULA

Caribbean Sea

MEXICO

CENTRAL AMERICA

Lake Nicaragua

SOUTH AMERICA

Isthmus of Panama

Equator

0   250   500 miles

0   250   500 kilometers

International boundary

▲ Mountain peak

N
W   E
S

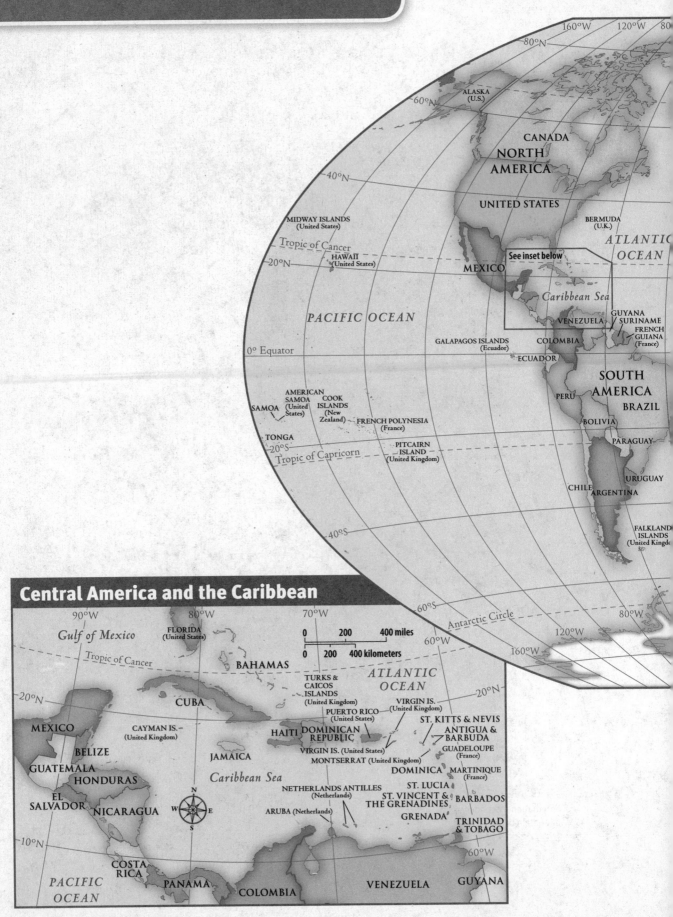

ALASKA
(U.S.)

CANADA

NORTH
AMERICA

UNITED STATES

BERMUDA
(U.K.)

ATLANTIC
OCEAN

MIDWAY ISLANDS
(United States)

Tropic of Cancer

HAWAII
(United States)

See inset below

MEXICO

Caribbean Sea

20°N

40°N

60°N

80°N

160°W   120°W   80

VENEZUELA

GUYANA
SURINAME
FRENCH
GUIANA
(France)

GALAPAGOS ISLANDS
(Ecuador)

COLOMBIA

ECUADOR

PACIFIC OCEAN

0° Equator

AMERICAN
SAMOA
(United
States)

COOK
ISLANDS
(New
Zealand)

SAMOA

FRENCH POLYNESIA
(France)

TONGA

PERU

SOUTH
AMERICA

BRAZIL

BOLIVIA

PARAGUAY

20°S

Tropic of Capricorn

PITCAIRN
ISLAND
(United Kingdom)

CHILE

URUGUAY

ARGENTINA

40°S

FALKLAND
ISLANDS
(United Kingdo

60°S

Antarctic Circle

60°W

80°W

120°W

160°W

Central America and the Caribbean

90°W   80°W   70°W

Gulf of Mexico

FLORIDA
(United States)

Tropic of Cancer

BAHAMAS

0   200   400 miles

0   200   400 kilometers

ATLANTIC
OCEAN

20°N

CUBA

TURKS &
CAICOS
ISLANDS
(United Kingdom)

PUERTO RICO
(United States)

VIRGIN IS.
(United Kingdom)

ST. KITTS & NEVIS

MEXICO

CAYMAN IS.
(United Kingdom)

HAITI

DOMINICAN
REPUBLIC

ANTIGUA &
BARBUDA

BELIZE

JAMAICA

VIRGIN IS. (United States)

GUADELOUPE
(France)

GUATEMALA

Caribbean Sea

MONTSERRAT (United Kingdom)

DOMINICA

MARTINIQUE
(France)

HONDURAS

NETHERLANDS ANTILLES
(Netherlands)

ST. LUCIA

EL
SALVADOR

NICARAGUA

N
W   E
S

ARUBA (Netherlands)

ST. VINCENT &
THE GRENADINES

BARBADOS

GRENADA

TRINIDAD
& TOBAGO

10°N

COSTA
RICA

PACIFIC
OCEAN

PANAMA

COLOMBIA

VENEZUELA

GUYANA

60°W

20°N

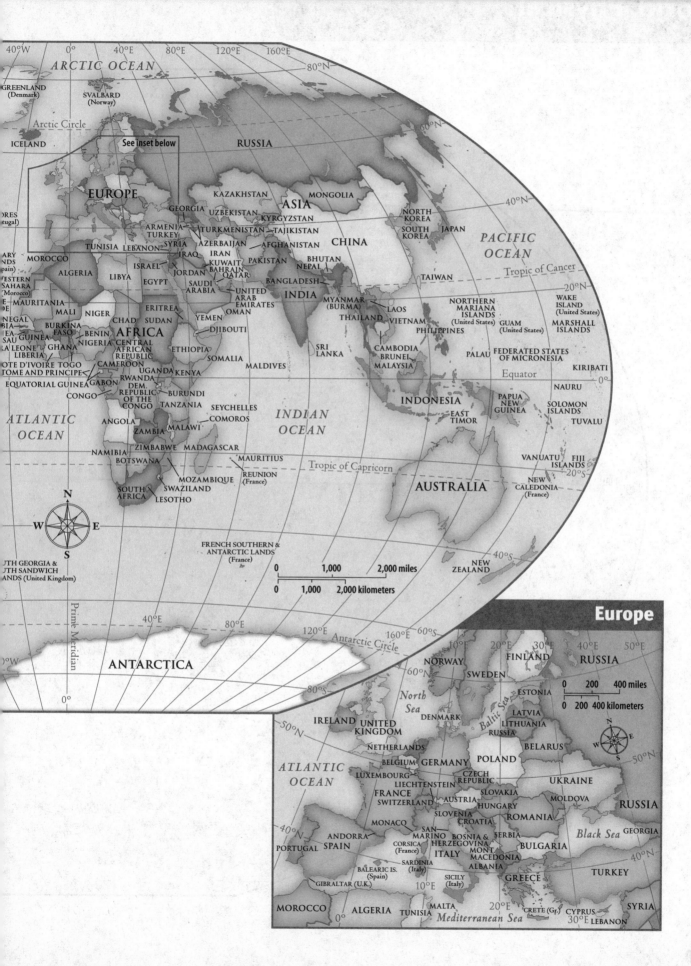

ARCTIC OCEAN

40°W 0° 40°E 80°E 120°E 160°E

80°N

GREENLAND
(Denmark)

SVALBARD
(Norway)

Arctic Circle

ICELAND

See inset below

RUSSIA

60°N

EUROPE

ORES
tugal)

ASIA 40°N

GEORGIA KAZAKHSTAN MONGOLIA

UZBEKISTAN KYRGYZSTAN

NORTH
KOREA

ARMENIA TURKMENISTAN TAJIKISTAN SOUTH JAPAN
TURKEY KOREA

PACIFIC
OCEAN

ARY
NDS
pain)

TUNISIA LEBANON SYRIA AZERBAIJAN AFGHANISTAN CHINA

MOROCCO IRAQ IRAN PAKISTAN BHUTAN TAIWAN Tropic of Cancer

ESTERN
SAHARA
(Morocco)

ALGERIA LIBYA ISRAEL JORDAN KUWAIT NEPAL 20°N
BAHRAIN
EGYPT SAUDI QATAR BANGLADESH WAKE
ARABIA UNITED INDIA ISLAND
ARAB (United States)

MAURITANIA EMIRATES MYANMAR NORTHERN
OMAN (BURMA) MARIANA GUAM MARSHALL
MALI NIGER ERITREA YEMEN LAOS ISLANDS (United States) ISLANDS
(United States)

CHAD SUDAN THAILAND VIETNAM
BURKINA DJIBOUTI
FASO BENIN AFRICA PHILIPPINES
NIGERIA CENTRAL ETHIOPIA SRI CAMBODIA FEDERATED STATES
AFRICAN LANKA PALAU OF MICRONESIA KIRIBATI
OTE D'IVOIRE TOGO REPUBLIC SOMALIA MALDIVES BRUNEI
TOME AND PRINCIPE CAMEROON MALAYSIA
UGANDA KENYA Equator NAURU
EQUATORIAL GUINEA GABON RWANDA
CONGO DEM. BURUNDI INDONESIA PAPUA
REPUBLIC NEW SOLOMON
OF THE TANZANIA GUINEA ISLANDS TUVALU
CONGO SEYCHELLES EAST
INDIAN TIMOR

ATLANTIC ANGOLA COMOROS OCEAN
OCEAN ZAMBIA MALAWI

NAMIBIA ZIMBABWE MADAGASCAR VANUATU FIJI
BOTSWANA MAURITIUS Tropic of Capricorn ISLANDS 20°S
MOZAMBIQUE REUNION AUSTRALIA NEW
SOUTH SWAZILAND (France) CALEDONIA
AFRICA LESOTHO (France)

N

W E

S

UTH GEORGIA &
UTH SANDWICH
ANDS (United Kingdom)

FRENCH SOUTHERN &
ANTARCTIC LANDS
(France)

0 1,000 2,000 miles

0 1,000 2,000 kilometers

40°S

NEW
ZEALAND

40°E 80°E 120°E 160°E 60°S

Antarctic Circle

0°W ANTARCTICA 80°S

0°

Europe

10°W 20°E 30°E 40°E 50°E

NORWAY FINLAND RUSSIA

60°N SWEDEN

0 200 400 miles

0 200 400 kilometers

North
Sea ESTONIA

N

IRELAND UNITED DENMARK LATVIA W E
KINGDOM LITHUANIA
RUSSIA S

NETHERLANDS BELARUS 50°N

ATLANTIC BELGIUM GERMANY POLAND
OCEAN LUXEMBOURG CZECH
LIECHTENSTEIN REPUBLIC UKRAINE
FRANCE SLOVAKIA
SWITZERLAND AUSTRIA MOLDOVA
HUNGARY ROMANIA RUSSIA
SLOVENIA
MONACO CROATIA Black Sea GEORGIA
ANDORRA SAN SERBIA BULGARIA
MARINO BOSNIA &
PORTUGAL SPAIN CORSICA HERZEGOVINA MONT. 40°N
(France) ITALY MACEDONIA TURKEY
SARDINIA ALBANIA
BALEARIC IS. (Italy) GREECE
(Spain) SICILY
GIBRALTAR (U.K.) (Italy) SYRIA

MOROCCO ALGERIA TUNISIA MALTA CRETE (Gr.) CYPRUS
0° 10°E 20°E 30°E LEBANON
Mediterranean Sea

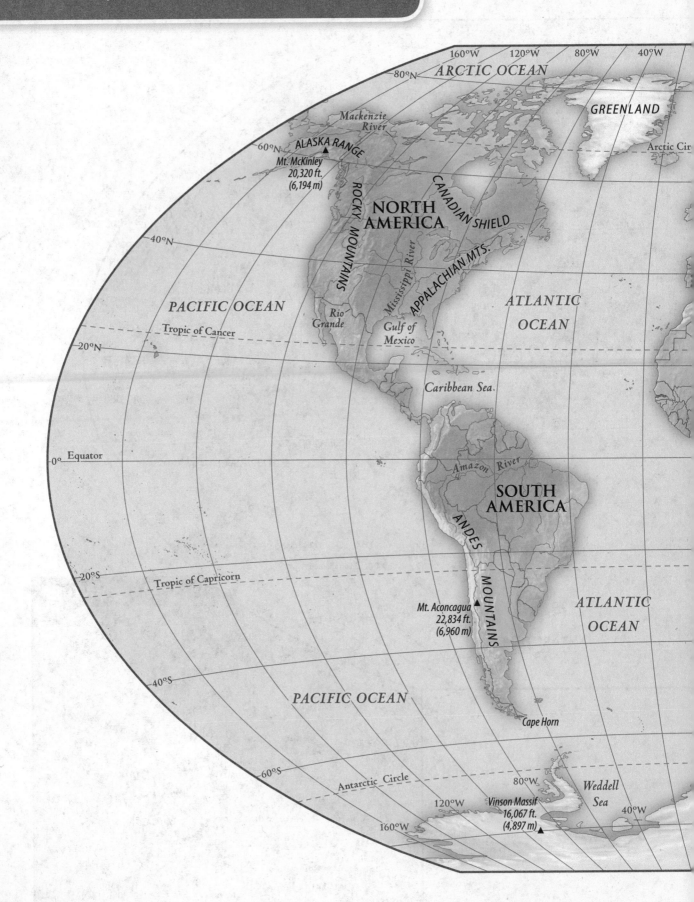

ARCTIC OCEAN

80°N

160°W 120°W 80°W 40°W

GREENLAND

Mackenzie River

60°N ALASKA RANGE

Arctic Cir

Mt. McKinley
20,320 ft.
(6,194 m)

ROCKY MOUNTAINS

NORTH
AMERICA

CANADIAN SHIELD

40°N

Mississippi River

APPALACHIAN MTS.

ATLANTIC
OCEAN

PACIFIC OCEAN

Tropic of Cancer

20°N

Rio
Grande

Gulf of
Mexico

Caribbean Sea

0° Equator

Amazon River

SOUTH
AMERICA

20°S Tropic of Capricorn

ANDES

Mt. Aconcagua
22,834 ft.
(6,960 m)

MOUNTAINS

ATLANTIC

OCEAN

40°S

PACIFIC OCEAN

Cape Horn

60°S

Antarctic Circle

80°W

Weddell
Sea

120°W Vinson Massif
16,067 ft.
(4,897 m)

40°W

160°W

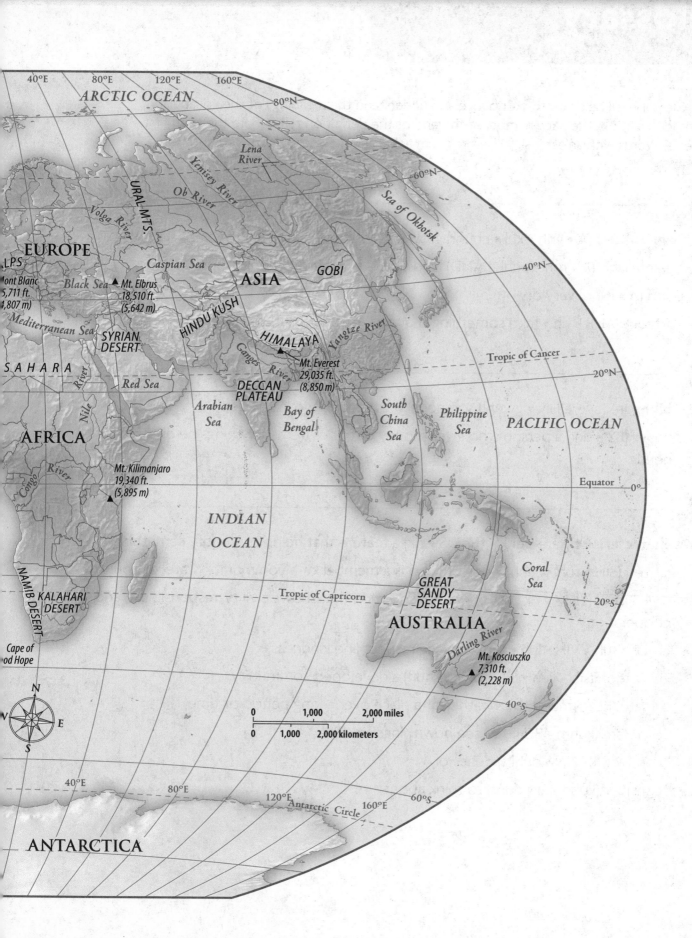

ARCTIC OCEAN

40°E 80°E 120°E 160°E 80°N

Lena River

Yenisey River

Ob River

URAL MTS.

Volga River

60°N

Sea of Okhotsk

EUROPE

Caspian Sea

ASIA GOBI

40°N

LPS

ont Blanc
5,711 ft.
4,807 m)

Black Sea ▲ Mt. Elbrus
18,510 ft.
(5,642 m)

HINDU KUSH

Mediterranean Sea

SYRIAN
DESERT

HIMALAYA

Yangtze River

Tropic of Cancer

SAHARA

River

Red Sea

Ganges River

▲ Mt. Everest
29,035 ft.
(8,850 m)

DECCAN
PLATEAU

20°N

Nile

Arabian
Sea

Bay of
Bengal

South
China
Sea

Philippine
Sea

PACIFIC OCEAN

AFRICA

Congo River

Mt. Kilimanjaro
19,340 ft.
(5,895 m)
▲

Equator 0°

INDIAN
OCEAN

NAMIB DESERT

KALAHARI
DESERT

Tropic of Capricorn

GREAT
SANDY
DESERT

Coral
Sea

20°S

AUSTRALIA

Cape of
od Hope

Darling River

Mt. Kosciuszko
7,310 ft.
(2,228 m)
▲

N

W E

S

40°S

0   1,000   2,000 miles

0   1,000   2,000 kilometers

40°E   80°E   120°E   160°E   60°S

Antarctic Circle

ANTARCTICA

R11

Glossary

This Glossary will help you to pronounce and understand the meanings of the vocabulary terms in this book. The page number at the end of the definition tells where the term first appears. Words with an asterisk (*) before them are academic vocabulary words.

A

agriculture (A • grih • kul • chuhr) growing crops and raising animals

arable land (A • ruh • buhl LAND) land that is good for growing crops

arid (A • ruhd) very dry

artifact (AHR • tih • fakt) something that was made or used by people in the past

B

bilingual (by • LIHN • gwuhl) someone who speaks two languages

buyer (BY • uhr) a person who gives money or trades items for things he or she wants or needs

C

characteristic (kare • ehk • tur • IS • tik) a feature that helps us identify something

citizen (SIH • tuh • zuhn) a person who is a member of a community, state, or country

civic virtue (SIH • vihk VUHR • choo) an action that shows civility, responsibility, and cooperation

civility (suh • VIH • luh • tee) showing respect and kindness

civilization (sih • vuh • luh • ZAY • shun) a developed community

climate (KLY • muht) the weather of a place over a long period of time

*compare (kuhm • PEHR) to see how things are alike

*conduct (KAHN • duhkt) behavior

*consider (kuhn • SI • duhr) to think about

Constitution (kahn • stuh • TOO • shuhn) a written plan for our government

continent (KAHN • tuh • nuhnt) one of the largest areas of land on Earth

contribution (kahn • truh • BYOO • shuhn) the act of giving or doing something

cooperation (koh • ah • puh • RAY • shuhn) working together to meet goals

council (KAUWN • suhl) a group of people who make the laws for a community

cuisine (kwih • ZEEN) style of cooking

culture (KUL • chuhr) a way of life shared by a group of people

currency (KUR • ehnt • see) a country's system of money

D

demand (dih • MAHND) the number of people who want or need something

distortion (dih • STAWR • shuhn) when an object loses its original size and shape

diversity (duh • VUHR • sih • tee) to have influences from many different cultures

E

economics (eh • kuh • NAH • miks) how money, goods, and services are produced and used

elevation (eh • luh • VAY • shuhn) the height of land above sea level

*entire (ehn • TY • uhr) all or whole

*establish (ih • STA • blish) to create, make, or form

exchange (ehks • CHAYNJ) when you trade or give up one item for another item

executive branch (ihg • ZEH • kyuh • tihv BRANCH) the branch of government that makes sure laws are followed

F

*feature (FEE • chur) a characteristic

*frame (FRAYM) a support or structure

Glossary

G

generation (jeh • nuh • RAY • shuhn) a group of people born and living around the same time

geography (jee • AH • gruh • fee) the study of Earth and the way living things use it

government (GUH • vuhrn • muhnt) all the people who run a community, state, or country

governor (GUH • vuhrn • uhr) leader of a state government

H

heritage (HEHR • uh • tihj) ways of life handed down from the past

history (HIS • tuh • ree) a study of events of the past

humidity (hyoo • MIH • duh • tee) the amount of water vapor in the air

I

*include (in • KLOOD) to cover or contain

J

judicial branch (joo • DIH • shuhl BRANCH) the branch of government that makes sure laws are carried out fairly

L

*label (LAY • buhl) to mark or tag

landform (LAND • fawrm) a shape on Earth's surface

legislative branch (LEH • juh • slay • tihv BRANCH) the branch of government that makes laws

*locate (LOH • kayt) to find

M

maritime climate (MEHR • uh • tym KLY • muht) climate controlled by a large body of water, such as an ocean

mayor (MAY • uhr) the leader of a local government

*model (MAH • duhl) a small copy of something

*method (MEH • thud) a plan for doing

O

*observe (uhb • ZUHRV) to witness or celebrate

P

*pattern (PA • tuhrn) a set of qualities that is repeated

peninsula (puh • NIHN • suh • luh) an area of land nearly surrounded by water

phosphate (FAHS • fayt) a mineral farmers use to help crops grow

plateau (pla • TOH) a high, flat area of land

President (PREH • zuh • duhnt) the leader of our country

*product (PRAH • duhkt) a good or item

R

*recall (rih • KAWL) to remember

recreation (reh • kree • AY • shuhn) the act of relaxing or playing for fun

region (REE • juhn) an area on Earth with common features

representative democracy (reh • prih • ZEHN • tuh • tihv dih • MAH • kruh • see) a government where the people vote for a group of leaders

Glossary

S

satellite image (SA • tuh • lyt IH • mihj) a picture of Earth taken from space

scarcity (SKEHR • suh • tee) when something is difficult to get or find

seller (SEH • luhr) a person who sells goods or services to other people

*style (STY • uhl) a way in which something is created

supply (suh • PLIH) the amount of something that is available

supreme (suh • PREEM) the most important

symbol (SYM • buhl) a picture that represents something else

T

trade (trayd) when you give one item in return for something else

tradition (truh • DIH • shuhn) a way of doing something that has been passed along by families for many years

transportation (trans • puhr • TAY • shuhn) a way of getting from one place to another

tundra (TUHN • druh) a treeless plain where only grasses and mosses can grow

V

vegetation (veh • juh • TAY • shuhn) plants that grow in an area

volunteer (vah • luhn • TIHR) a person who chooses to do something without getting paid

Index

This index lists many topics that appear in the book, along with the pages on which they are found. Page numbers after an *m* refer to a map. Page numbers after a *p* refer to a photograph or picture. Page numbers after a *c* refer to a chart or diagram. Page numbers after a *g* refer to a graph.

Index

Index

Index